PREDATORY TRADING
AND CROWDED EXITS

NEW THINKING ON MARKET VOLATILITY

BY JAMES CLUNIE

James Clunie

Nelly Terekhova

HARRIMAN HOUSE LTD

3A Penns Road
Petersfield
Hampshire
GU32 2EW
GREAT BRITAIN

Tel: +44 (0)1730 233870
Fax: +44 (0)1730 233880
Email: enquiries@harriman-house.com
Website: www.harriman-house.com

First published in Great Britain in 2010

The right of James Clunie to be identified as the author has been asserted
in accordance with the Copyright, Design and Patents Act 1988.

978-1-906659-05-9

British Library Cataloguing in Publication Data
A CIP catalogue record for this book can be obtained from the British Library.

Printed and bound in the UK by CPI Antony Rowe, Chippenham

Contents

About the Author

James Clunie works at Scottish Widows Investment Partnership (SWIP), where he is responsible for managing a UK equity long-short fund and a long-only fund. Previously, he was at the University of Edinburgh for four years, conducting research into stock lending and short-selling. He also set up and ran their Masters programme in Finance and Investment. Prior to this, Clunie worked at Murray Johnstone International, where he was head of asset allocation, and at Aberdeen Asset Management, where he was head of global equities. He graduated with a BSc (Hons) in Mathematics and Statistics and recently completed his PhD on indirect short-selling constraints, both at the University of Edinburgh. He is a chartered financial analyst.

Acknowledgements

I would like to thank Stephen Eckett for suggesting that I write this book and for his effective editing work. I would also like to thank Suzanne Anderson for guiding me through the publishing process. It has been a pleasure to work with each member of the team at Harriman House on this project.

Special thanks go to Nelly Terekhova for her research assistance on this book.

Thanks to Yuan Gao and Tatiana Pyatigorskaya for their assistance in building and analysing the dataset used to examine short-sellers' behaviour. Also, thanks to Charalambos Constantinou for his work in analysing index fund predation and to Mariam Megvinetuhutsesi for her assistance in researching the ethics of predatory trading.

I am grateful to Will Duff Gordon at Data Explorers Ltd and Catherine Somers at Datastream Ltd. for providing valuable data for this research. I am also grateful to the quantitative research team at Macquarie and to Neil Heywood at Matrix Trading Systems, each of whom gave me permission to use their research findings on the use of stop losses.

I would like to thank all those who agreed to be interviewed for aspects of my research. Finally, thanks to reviewers and participants at the Midwest Finance Association conference in Chicago (March, 2009), the European Financial Management conference in Nantes (April, 2009), the State Street Risk Forum (2007), the Edinburgh University Centre for Financial Markets Research (2008), the JP Morgan Quantitative Conference (2008) and the CFA/INQUIRE seminar in London (February, 2009) for their helpful ideas and suggestions on research that was used in this book.

Preface

What this book is about

In this book I look at a series of phenomena that can drive security prices temporarily away from their equilibrium levels, creating opportunities for traders to profit from. At the same time, these phenomena create the risk of losses for the unaware.

The phenomena I examine have only recently begun to be better understood. They include two important liquidity problems faced by traders: predatory trading and crowded exits. I examine these on three levels. Firstly, I describe the basic principles and theory behind the phenomena, to build a solid framework for the way we think about these situations. Secondly, I examine the accumulated empirical evidence on these events. This reveals what has generally happened in these situations, and what the profit opportunity and risks might be like. Finally, I consider a number of individual cases to illustrate what can happen to traders in practice. In the main, these will be extreme events or special situations from which we can learn.

By understanding these phenomena in this way a trader could gain an edge over others in the market. In the first instance, this is achieved by avoiding becoming the victim of the phenomena I describe. Beyond this, it might be possible to use detailed knowledge of some of these situations to (legally and ethically) profit from the events.

Who this book is for

This book should be of interest to traders seeking to gain a superior understanding of how markets work, both in theory and in practice. It should also be of interest to longer-horizon investors who are seeking to avoid timing errors, and to risk managers seeking to understand better the subtleties of risk beyond traditional risk statistics. Finally, I expect that a number of academics and students of markets will find this work stimulating and thought-provoking.

How the book is structured

The book starts with an introduction to the notion of the 'fair value' of a security. Then, by thinking of markets as an eco-system of different types of players, I describe ways in which securities prices can move away from equilibrium and stay mis-priced for some time. I examine specific examples of these phenomena, include predatory trading, the use of stop losses, crowded exits and manipulation. I end with some thoughts on how traders should make use of their knowledge of these phenomena.

Introduction

Imagine the following situation. You are a trader who understands the relationship between two similar assets. That relationship appears out of line with its historical pattern and little has changed in the way of fundamentals over the past few months. You place the trade, hedging one asset against the other. Now, you only need to wait for convergence...

But it doesn't happen.

The trade moves the other way and you are now nursing a painful loss. No matter, you think, the fundamentals remain unchanged and the trade now looks more attractive than ever. You even try to encourage convergence by advertising the attractiveness of this position to other traders.

But then your position falls to an even greater loss. You are reminded of your head trader's favourite piece of advice:

The market will move to the point that causes the maximum pain

It's beginning to feel that way. If the trade diverges any further you will be stopped out by your own risk controls.

The trade continues to diverge, the pain builds and you are indeed stopped out.

A few days later you see that the two assets have moved sharply back towards their historical relationship. You were correct in your original analysis. But somehow the market had conspired to impose swingeing losses on you.

How did this happen?

Every trader should have a thorough understanding of phenomena such as predatory trading and manipulation; and of liquidity problems that can arise when traders position themselves in a similar fashion to one another. These problems are often understood intuitively, but there is a benefit from understanding the theory behind them and from seeing the evidence of how they work.

In this book, after setting the scene in the first chapter, I look at predatory trading, crowded exits, stop losses and manipulation. In each case, I consider the risks and opportunities that arise for traders.

CHAPTER 1

THE ECOLOGY OF MARKETS

Fair value

What is the right price for an asset?

A common way of thinking about this problem for a security, such as a stock or a bond, is in terms of its fair value. This is the notion that there is a single value that the security is intrinsically worth at any given time.

A rigorous way in which to think about the intrinsic value of a security is to consider the future cash flows that the security will generate for the owner, and then discount those cash flows back to today's money. This concept relies on the idea that an expected cash flow at some future date is less valuable than money in hand today, because of the opportunity cost of not having access to the cash today, and the risks associated with future events. Where an investor or trader knows the future cash flows from a security for certain, and knows the rate at which to discount them, calculating the fair value of that security is simple – a few lines of work on a spreadsheet.

But, in practice, things are not so easy.

Consider, for example, a bond issued by a highly credit-worthy government. The cash flows are documented in the bond's prospectus and are known almost with certainty: each regular coupon payment and the return of principal at maturity of the bond are highly likely to transpire. So far, so simple.

But what is the correct discount rate?

Ambiguity over the appropriate discount rate makes it difficult in practice to estimate the fair value of a security. Analysts develop techniques for coping with this problem – one of the most popular of which is taking the implied discount rate from similar securities, and using this to discount the cash flows from the security in question.

Now consider a riskier security, such as a corporate bond. In this case, the cash flows to the bond's owner are less certain, as default risk is now higher. Consequently, the intrinsic value of a corporate bond is thus (generally) more difficult to evaluate than for a government bond.

And difficulties do not end with corporate bonds.

Equities offer greater problems – think about the unreliability of cash flows and dividends attributable to shareholders. An extreme example would be, say, a biotechnology company, where cash flows might be zero for the foreseeable future and in the long-run might depend upon success in developing new drugs. Long-term cash flows could be huge...or non-existent!

Uncertainty over both cash flows and the appropriate discount rates leads to great uncertainty over the fair value of a security. Two analysts, each using the same theoretical discounted cash-flow approach, could place very different values on the same security, depending on their cash-flow projections and the discount rates they choose to use. Because of such ambiguity over the true value of a security, some analysts dismiss the notion of a fair value. Instead, they think of securities as having observed market prices and estimated cash flows, and simply use the implied discount rate in the market to compare securities to one another.

Many financial models assume a fair value exists

Whether or not it is sensible in practice to think about the fair value of a security, a number of financial models *assume* that there is such a thing as the fair value of a security. A quick trawl through published articles and working papers on asset pricing reveals that this is a very popular assumption in academic work. Some models go further still: not only do they assume that there is a fair value to a security, but this fair value is known with certainty to some market actors, such as arbitrageurs. But how do the arbitrageurs *know* the fair value of a security? Most papers are mute on this subject.

Why would a model-builder make such an assumption?

Mainly because it creates a framework for thinking about markets which, through further analysis, can provide illumination on how markets work. The assumption that fair value can be known with certainty might come as a surprise to some arbitrageurs. To know the fair value for say, a stock, seems like a hopelessly unrealistic assumption. However, academic work sometimes makes simplifying assumptions, to reduce the complexity of a situation, and to make the mathematics more tractable.

According to Friedman (1953), the use of unrealistic assumptions does not invalidate the work, so long as the predictions are accurate. Thus, the notion of a fair value that is known to some, but not all, market actors is a simplifying assumption to help us understand the actions of arbitrageurs and the workings of markets. It is worth bearing this in mind when looking at financial models that rely upon such assumptions. Models can provide illumination on how markets work, but a trader must avoid the mistake of relying wholly upon the predictions of models.

The problem of simplifying assumptions

Some asset-pricing models make a further, important simplifying assumption about the process of arbitrage. They assume that traders can short-sell securities as easily as they can buy. For example, a widely-taught asset pricing model, known as the arbitrage theory of capital asset pricing (Ross, 1976), assumes that there are no restrictions on short-sales, including full use of the short-sale proceeds. However, in practice, short-sellers must find securities to borrow, effectively pay securities lending fees and face collateralisation and margin requirements. These short-sale constraints limit the frequency and scope of arbitrage, and so could affect the price of assets.

So, we know that some models that seek to explain the pricing of assets make use of unrealistic simplifying assumptions.

Does this matter?

Are the predictions from such models accurate, or do they instead fail the 'Friedman test' that I mentioned earlier? In a canonical paper on short-selling constraints, Miller (1977) considers what happens to security prices if the two main assumptions discussed above are untrue at the same time.

While popular models such as the capital asset pricing model (see Sharpe, 1964) assume that investors have identical estimates of the expected return and probability distribution of returns from all securities, Miller suggests that investors in practice can have differing expectations about securities instead, due to uncertainty over future cash flows and the appropriate discount rate for an investment. He argues that when a divergence of opinion amongst investors is combined with barriers to short-selling, the price of a security is no longer set by the average investor, but instead by the beliefs of the most optimistic investors. Those investors with the most optimistic estimates of returns will own the securities, while pessimists and realists struggle to short-sell the overpriced asset because of constraints on short-selling. Miller concludes that

> the presence of a substantial number of well informed investors
> will prevent there from being substantially undervalued securities,

but there may be securities whose price has been bid up to excessive levels by an uninformed minority.

This provides a simple explanation for why some securities might trade at inflated prices. Even if informed traders or investors know the fair value of a security, other less-informed traders push the price beyond that level, and it is difficult to short-sell the security back to its fair price. Mis-pricing develops because of ambiguity over fair value; and arbitrageurs are unable to correct the anomaly if there are barriers to short-selling.

A number of researchers have investigated Miler's idea. Although there is some dispute over its implications, Asquith *et al.* (2005) state

> that it is now widely accepted that if short-selling is costly and there are heterogeneous investor beliefs, a stock can be overvalued and generate low subsequent returns.

For a trader, the lesson is simple – asset pricing models can help us understand how markets work, but where the model relies upon simplifying assumptions, the predictions from the models might not always be accurate. A good trader should understand both the *predictions* of the model and the *limitations* of the model. Without both, a trader will be vulnerable – even if this vulnerability takes years to be revealed.

Informed traders versus noise traders

A noise trader is simply a trader who holds no new information about a security. Any knowledge upon which he trades is assumed to be already imputed in the security's price. Given this definition, it might seem that noise traders would be largely irrelevant to the functioning of markets. However, Gemmill and Thomas (2002) argue that the setting of prices in a market is determined through the interactions of arbitrageurs and noise traders. Furthermore, many models for understanding how security prices are set are based on the notion that a market comprises informed traders (those who know the fair value of a security) and noise traders (those who do not know).

Who are these noise traders?

Although rarely made explicit, noise traders are implicitly assumed to include non-professional traders (e.g. retail investors) – even though it is likely that at least some retail investors have better investing track records than some professionals. Noise traders might also include traders forced to trade because of a need for liquidity. Dow and Gorton (2006) argue that "noise traders play an important role in modern finance theory", but state that their "identities, motivations and ability to persist" are not well understood.

In other words, we do not know much about a group of people that we believe plays an important role in the workings of markets. This is quite some confession!

Noise traders can have both benign and adverse effects on markets. Black (1986) argues that with more noise trading, markets will be more liquid, in the sense of having frequent trades that allow prices to be observed. However, security prices will reflect both the information upon which information-traders trade, but also the noise upon which noise-traders trade.

As noise trading increases, information trading becomes more profitable, because of the greater noise contained in prices. However, apparent 'information' may already be reflected in security prices, making it difficult to differentiate information from noise. Noise can create the opportunity for profitable trading, but simultaneously makes it difficult to trade profitably.

Even without short-sale constraints, the existence of noise trading means that securities need not be rationally priced, and arbitrage becomes risky. Information can give a

> " We do not know much about a group of people that we believe plays an important role in the workings of markets. "

trader an edge, but not a guaranteed profit. Consequently, informed traders will not take large enough (i.e. risky enough) positions to eliminate the noise.

Black surmises that it will be difficult to show that information-traders perform better than noise-traders, and argues:

> there will always be a lot of ambiguity about who is an information trader and who is a noise trader.

Noise traders, through their uninformed trades, can set up mis-pricing opportunities for better-informed traders to exploit. But noise traders can also *overwhelm* informed traders, if their scale is large and they trade in a similar fashion to one another.

Noise traders should thus be applauded for creating opportunities for traders, but also feared when they move as a pack. Superior knowledge alone is not enough to guarantee success as a trader. We know from financial history that even well-informed arbitrageurs can be quite vulnerable.

Why smart arbitrageurs don't always win...

Shleifer and Vishny (1997) describe one of the ways in which a well-informed arbitrageur can fail. A textbook description of arbitrage suggests that the process requires no capital, entails no risk and generates guaranteed and immediate profits. This kind of arbitrage would bring prices towards equilibrium and keep markets efficient.

However, the authors argue that:

> the textbook description does not describe realistic arbitrage trades and, moreover, the discrepancies become particularly important when arbitrageurs manage other people's money.

Types of arbitrage that appear to be simple, such as that between two similar bond futures contracts traded on different exchanges, can take on the characteristics of risk arbitrage when considered fully. Even mechanically hedged arbitrage positions, such as long stock/short future, can result in financial distress if the arbitrageur earns paper profits on the stock leg but is unable to meet the cash requirements arising from losses on the futures leg. Risk arbitrage bears risk of loss and requires capital – an important distinction from the textbook definition of arbitrage.

> **Superior knowledge alone is not enough to guarantee success as a trader.**

The role of clients

Furthermore, the model of arbitrage assumed in many popular asset pricing models is inconsistent with how arbitrage is practised in financial markets. Instead of vast numbers of small arbitrageurs, arbitrage is conducted in practice by relatively few specialised professionals, who generally use outsiders' money to take large positions. An agency relationship thus exists between the specialised arbitrageurs and their clients. Where a prospective client seeks to place money with a hedge fund but has a limited knowledge or experience of arbitrage, he might simply allocate capital to those funds with the strongest track records. Consequently, the size of funds under management becomes related to the past performance of the arbitrageur.

This dynamic can generate some interesting outcomes for markets. As an illustration, assume the existence of noise traders, so that securities need not be *always* rationally priced. Idiosyncratic risk (risk that cannot be hedged) can deter arbitrageurs. Consequently, securities with idiosyncratic risk can remain mis-priced for some time. With the existence of noise traders, arbitrage positions can widen and the arbitrageur loses money. Some clients might react to these losses by seeking to redeem their fund assets. However, if we assume that any market mis-pricings will eventually be corrected, the expected returns from arbitrage positions are high exactly when past returns are low. Thus, arbitrageurs can be forced to close positions that offer high expected returns, exacerbating deviations from equilibrium.

The poor performance of many classes of hedge fund during 2008 was followed by large client redemptions, and presumably the closure of some attractive arbitrage positions. In so far as this created deviations from equilibrium, those traders with capital to deploy and an ability to spot the mis-pricings would find such a trading environment very fertile. For those risk-arbitrageurs who suffered redemptions, the need to liquidate attractive positions must have been a galling experience.

Where the price of a security moves far away from an estimate of its fundamental value, one might expect it to revert at some future point. But simply identifying a mis-priced security is not enough. It could remain over-priced for some time or the mis-pricing could even grow, resulting in losses and ultimately redemptions for the arbitrageur. The path the security price takes is important, because some market players might be unable to hold onto positions that produce losses.

Hedge funds attempt to mitigate the risk of clients redeeming in response to losses by using devices such as 'lock-in periods' and 'gates' that impose contractual restrictions on clients seeking to withdraw funds. However, potential clients might fear being locked in to a poorly performing fund and so it could be more difficult to promote and market this type of fund. Only managers with strong track records are likely to be able to persuade clients to accept lengthy lock-in periods.

Educating clients about the need to hold on to attractive positions after losses is another important, albeit time-intensive, initiative to minimise redemption risk. Arguably, the best time to do this is when returns have been strong and the client can understand the principle of holding on to attractive positions that have experienced near-term losses. If education is left to the last minute, when the losses start appearing, there is a higher risk that the client's emotions will overwhelm the discussion.

Delayed arbitrage

Another way that arbitrageurs can deal with noise trader risk is via delayed arbitrage. This is discussed in an article by Abreu and Brunermeier (2002). They build a model for arbitrage that considers uncertainty about the market timing decisions of other rational arbitrageurs, and thus the timing of the price correction. They call this problem synchronisation risk. The model shows that rational arbitrageurs do not act immediately on knowledge of security over-valuation, but instead wait for other rational arbitrageurs to learn about the over-valuation. Acting immediately might lead to losses, if enough other rational arbitrageurs do not know of the over-valuation and fail to act at the same time.

The lesson from this model for traders is clear: arbitrage is more than just identifying mis-priced assets. A good short-seller should combine knowledge of mis-pricings with a catalyst. In this case, the catalyst is knowledge that other traders are about to short the security too. This concept of delayed arbitrage can help explain why apparently obvious

market bubbles can
continue to grow.
Short-sellers, the very
people who might be

❝ Arbitrage is more than just identifying mis-priced assets. ❞

expected to prick the bubble and bring over-valued securities back into line, can be absent when they are needed most. And they would be absent for good reason – they want to avoid being overwhelmed by a tidal wave of optimistic noise traders.

Tidal waves and market bubbles

Such tidal waves of noise trading emerge much as fads and fashions do. Where market participants obtain information and opinions from the same source, or share opinions with one another on websites or other media, noise traders can begin to believe in a common story, to imitate one another's trading and to herd in their behaviour. As momentum builds, a fashion can develop into a bubble.

One of the most famous purported market bubbles from recent years involved the rapid ascent in technology, media and telecom (TMT) stocks from around 1998 through to March 2000 and their subsequent sharp decline (March 2000 – March 2003). Brunnermeier and Nagel investigated the activities of hedge funds around the time of this ascent and collapse in TMT stock prices. Their article was published in 2004, by which time the NASDAQ index had fallen over 75% from its peak of March 2000 and just about everyone grounded in realism agreed that the TMT stock phenomenon of the late 1990s had been a bubble.

One might expect that hedge funds were trying to short-sell egregiously over-valued TMT stocks in 1999 and early 2000, but the authors found that hedge funds were in aggregate *over-weighted* in technology stocks in 1999 and early 2000.

Why might this have been?

These hedge fund positions cannot be explained by barriers to short-selling: if short-selling was too difficult or too costly, a fund would simply hold a zero position in the security, or at the very least some under-weighted position relative to the benchmark weight of the security. Funds would certainly not have held over-weighted positions if they believed that the shares were about to fall in price. This notion is reinforced by a separate study by Geczy *et al.* (2002) that found that short exposure to dotcom stocks was neither costly nor difficult during this period.

In light of this evidence, Brunnermeier and Nagel concluded that hedge funds were 'riding the technology bubble', rather than short-selling apparently over-valued stocks. In a market with many optimistic noise traders, it might not pay to immediately short-sell over-valued stocks. Informed traders almost certainly knew that TMT stocks were over-valued, but feared the army of optimistic 'new paradigm' noise traders enough to stay well away from shorting TMT stocks...for years on end!

Don't be a hero!

The advice for traders tempted to short-sell assets that appear to be in a bubble is to avoid any isolated, heroic action. Sit it out until the tide turns, or (for the thrill-seeking) join in and ride the bubble, while keeping a very close eye on the exit door!

A number of high-profile investors and traders ignored this advice and paid the price with their jobs or funds. Amongst the best known victims of synchronisation risk and TMT noise trader madness were Julian Robertson at Tiger Asset Management, who closed his investment company in March 2000 after incurring losses; and, amongst long-only portfolio managers, value investor Tony Dye, chief investment officer at Phillips & Drew asset management in London, whose employment ended only three days before the peak of the market.

Reverse broking

Traders can find shortcuts to the problem of synchronisation risk. In practice, arbitrageurs can enter immediately into seemingly attractive positions and then proceed to advise their known contacts, such as brokers and peers, of the attractiveness of that position. This is sometimes known as 'reverse broking'. In their observational study of a hedge fund, Hardie and MacKenzie (2007) observed the following situation:

> The trader asked his assistant to construct a spreadsheet of recent prices of the two bonds, which supported the view that it was indeed an anomaly and thus a trading opportunity. Having first made the necessary purchases and short sales to take advantage of it, the trader then phoned a contact in an investment bank to direct his attention to the anomaly – 'There is at least half a point in that trade, and there is zero market risk' – and sent him the spreadsheet.

The purpose of this activity is to encourage dissemination of the idea and to alert other arbitrageurs to the opportunity. This has two effects: first, it lowers the risk of greater divergence of the position from fair value, so limiting margin calls and the risk of performance-based arbitrage. Secondly, it might bring the trades of other actors forward in time, thus reducing synchronisation risk. This suggests a social dimension to arbitrage, well beyond simply identifying mis-priced securities. Where such reverse broking is based on the interpretation of factual information (as opposed to false rumours) it is an entirely legitimate activity.

More complicated worlds

So far, we have considered a very simple world, populated only by informed arbitrageurs and uninformed noise traders. And yet this simple world has already led to a better understanding of arbitrage and risk, and has allowed for the development of bubbles.

What happens if we add in other market actors?

One example of a more complicated model is provided by De Long *et al.* (1990) who create a model with two assets: cash and stock. There are three types of traders: positive feedback traders, fundamental-versus-price-comparator investors and utility-maximising informed rational speculators.

- **Positive feedback traders** simply buy stock after its price has risen, and sell after its price falls. They are associated with price momentum trading or trend following, stop-loss orders (selling a risky asset after a price drop below some pre-defined level), dynamic hedging (selling a risky asset after a price fall, and vice versa), and the liquidation of positions by investors unable to meet margin calls.

- **Fundamental-versus-price comparator investors** are simply disciplined 'value' investors. They acquire stock when it trades below its assumed fundamental value and sell stock when it rises above its assumed fundamental value.

- **Informed rational speculators,** on learning some news about a security, not only trade in response to the news, but also trade additionally in anticipation of the positive feedback traders' response to the rational speculator's trading. Stock price movements in response to news thus become exaggerated.

The model reveals patterns of stock prices that are consistent with the empirical evidence of positive serial correlation of returns over periods of weeks or months (i.e. price momentum), followed by mean reversion over several years. Such patterns could also be obtained without anticipatory trading by rational speculators, so long as positive feedback traders operate in the market. The authors argue that in the presence of positive feedback traders, it might be rational for investors to "jump on the bandwagon and not buck the trend" when prices are trending. This is exactly the sort of behaviour that Brunnermeier and Nagel found amongst hedge funds around the time of the TMT stock bubble.

The ecology of markets

Why build a model with only two or three types of actor? There is nothing to stop us from considering more realistic models, if these aid our understanding. We know that markets can contain index trackers, value investors, market makers, momentum traders, dynamic hedgers and many other participants. Together, these various parties make up the ecology of a market.

This way of thinking about markets is not yet dominant in the academic community, but has the support of a small number of influential thinkers. Perhaps it is the mathematical difficulty in modelling so many different types of agent that prevents its wider adoption.

Thinking about markets in ecological terms builds on work in sociobiology[1] and involves the application of evolutionary ideas to social interactions. Thinking about financial transactions in this way is

---

[1] See Wilson, 1975.

an alternative to the use of equilibrium models. Ormerod (2005) argues that equilibrium models, much admired in economics literature, are unrealistic in light of the actual behaviour of markets. Bernstein (1998) argues that evolutionary processes better explain the workings of markets than does the notion of equilibrium.

In currency markets, for example, it is common for traders to talk about the ecology of markets. It is widely accepted that two major types of players are not motivated by profit and so can create opportunities for others to exploit. First among these are a number of central banks that intervene from time to time in the markets in an attempt to hold their own currencies at desired relative levels, in accordance with national economic or trade policy. Secondly, some international industrial firms hedge their foreign exchange exposures as a risk control measure, rather than as a profit-maximising measure. Arguably, the ecology of the currency markets is such that it provides opportunities for traders to earn profits at the expense of non-profit-motivated actors.

Sociobiological ideas can be seen in any research that involves studying the survival rates of certain types of traders. For example, Hirschleifer and Luo (2001) examine the long-term prospects of over-confident traders within a securities market – a study into the survival of a flawed species of market actor. Arguably, when economists discuss business cycles and the creative destruction of capitalism, they are expressing evolutionary thoughts about markets.

In his book, *Education of a Speculator*, Victor Niederhoffer (1997) writes about markets as a collection of different players. He thinks in terms of an ecology of markets and defines ecology as "the study of the webs that link the players [in the various markets]". He argues that "slow-moving participants" such as the general public provide the losses or "energy source" upon which dealers, brokers and large hedge funds feed. He also explains how security prices can temporarily move

away from their
equilibrium
values as a result
of the activities
of trend-
followers who

❝ Evolutionary processes better explain the workings of markets than does the notion of equilibrium. ❞

use stop losses to protect themselves from unlimited losses, and of dealers who hedge their options exposure.

Niederhoffer argues that the influence of prices in other markets and the behaviour of contrarian and value investors provides "homeostatic negative feedback" to any given market and helps to keep prices near to equilibrium value. His rich description of markets will be much more familiar to traders and investors than the simple asset pricing models that I discussed earlier. Of course, modelling such a complex eco-system can be difficult, and it is for this reason that many-asset pricing models consider only a small number of actors.

Some of the players in a market eco-system attempt to estimate the intrinsic value of securities. They place trades in an attempt to exploit apparent divergences from intrinsic value. A value investor would be the simplest example of such a player. By contrast, a momentum trader might follow trends in returns regardless of fundamentals, in the expectation that those trends will continue. Others players appear to have little interest in either value or momentum.

Consider, for example, a full replication index fund that must trade to match changes to a benchmark; or a retail investor who must sell securities at the prevailing market price to help finance a house purchase. Lo (2004) argues that:

> because human behaviour is heuristic, adaptive, and not
> completely predictable – at least not nearly to the same extent as
> physical phenomena – modelling the joint behaviour of many

individuals is far more challenging than modelling just one individual. Indeed, the behaviour of even a single individual can be baffling at times, as each of us has surely experienced on occasion.

Nevertheless, we should be able to achieve a better understanding of markets by studying how different players interact with one another. Agent-based modelling of markets[2] attempts to describe the developing behaviour and interaction of market participants, by defining the behaviour of agents and simulating outcomes amongst them. These models show that prices fluctuate with internal dynamics caused by the interaction of diverse trading strategies. They need not necessarily reflect true values.

Ever-changing cycles

Patterns in prices that appear in one period tend to disappear as agents learn of the predictable behaviour of others and evolve profitable strategies to exploit them. However, these evolutions take time and apparent price anomalies may persist. New patterns may also appear over time. Such phenomena have also been observed in actual markets. For example, Niederhoffer writes:

> results that appeared significant in one period had a tendency to evaporate in subsequent periods. If a phenomenon truly exists, shrewd operators discover it and start anticipating it in following periods, thereby evening out the moves.

He calls this the phenomenon of 'ever-changing cycles', which makes it difficult to establish technical trading rules or to develop algorithmic trading strategies based on academic research. That is, the ecology of markets is in constant flux.

---

[2] See, for example, Arthur *et al.* (1997); Farmer and Lo (1999).

Adaptive markets

Lo (2004) introduces the adaptive markets hypothesis, in which the "dynamics of evolution – competition, mutation, reproduction and natural selection – determine the efficiency of markets" and the success or otherwise of investment strategies. The author argues that many of the common apparent mistakes made by investors (such as the tendency of investors to avoid realising losses) can be explained by "an evolutionary model of individuals adapting to a changing environment via simple heuristics."

If we think of markets in this way, then survival can become more important to a trader than maximising expected utility within a rational-expectations framework. Traders learn, through trial and error and natural selection, rules or heuristics for survival. In a relatively stable environment, these heuristics adapt to become roughly optimal solutions. If economic conditions change, there is a risk that such heuristics became maladaptive. Markets history matters, through the forces of natural selection. Furthermore, aggregate risk preferences are path dependent under this

> **"** Models show that prices fluctuate with internal dynamics caused by the interaction of diverse trading strategies. They need not necessarily reflect true values. **"**

framework. Arbitrage opportunities do exist from time to time. As economic conditions change, new markets are created, new species emerge and others die out. Investment strategies will vary in successfulness, depending on the economic environment and market ecology.

How does this ecological view of markets relate to more traditional perspectives?

According to Lo, the notion of efficient markets concerns "the steady-state limit of a population with constant environmental conditions" and behavioural finance concerns "specific adaptations of certain groups that may or may not persist, depending on the particular evolutionary paths that the economy experiences". Thus, the adaptive markets hypothesis can reconcile many of the apparent contradictions between the two dominant views on how prices are set.

The high mortality rate for hedge funds can be understood better by considering them as a species within the market eco-system. Prolonged negative returns hinder their economic viability and can lead to the exit, or death, of the hedge fund. By knowing who is vulnerable, who is making mistakes and from where your next meal is likely to come, the trader builds up an edge within the market eco-system.

In particular, good knowledge of popular strategies employed in the market, and an understanding of any behavioural anomalies in other agents, is required. Each player attempts to exploit the behaviour of others. In the short-run, optimal portfolio allocation rules depend on the ecology of the market, but in the long-run, under-diversified portfolios can be driven out by a small group of invading agents.

Cross-market trading

There is no need to confine our thinking to just one market. We can envisage a market eco-system that includes not only different types of capital instrument, but also derivatives and markets in different countries.

Strategies such as capital-structure arbitrage, for example, involve trading across more than one market in the securities of a single company. It could, for example, involve buying bonds issued by a company but selling equity in that same company.

> **"** By knowing who is vulnerable, who is making mistakes and from where your next meal is likely to come, the trader builds up an edge within the market eco-system. **"**

Although designed to exploit arbitrage anomalies between markets, these strategies can be risky. Yu (2006) examined the expected returns and risks from capital structure arbitrage and found that significant losses occur with alarming frequency. Ofek *et al.* (2004) have examined violations of 'put-call parity', a 'no-arbitrage' relationship that one expects to hold in options markets. These violations represent a pricing anomaly between equity and option markets and should be arbitraged away soon after they arise, subject to some of the constraints on arbitrage and risks that we have discussed already.

But why should such cross market anomalies arise in the first instance?

One possible explanation is that there is segmentation between the equity and options market – in other words, some players are confined to only one market. For example, a long-only equity investment fund may not be permitted to trade in options. Such constrained players could actually exacerbate pricing anomalies between markets, if forced to trade within a single market segment regardless of price because of, say, client redemptions. Furthermore, they would be unable to correct pricing anomalies between markets through arbitrage.

For traders and risk arbitrageurs, this suggests that cross-market flexibility is important for maximising the opportunity set.

Free money

Examples of cross market anomalies abound. A notable case involves the issuance on 31 October, 2008 by the British bank, Barclays plc, of £4.3 billion of new mandatory convertible notes (MCNs) in an effort to raise additional tier-one capital during the economic slowdown that year. The MCNs were issued at more than a 22% price discount to the ordinary shares and yet offered a higher yield and a fixed conversion price (subject to adjustment clauses for any future equity issuance below the MCN conversion price). The discount offered by the MCNs created a clear arbitrage opportunity against the equities of the firm.

There was also good liquidity in Barclays' ordinary shares – the third panel of Figure 1.1 below shows that there was elevated trading volume in the ordinary shares on the day of issuance of the MCNs, with approximately £200 million traded. On 31 October, the firm's ordinary shares initially *rose* sharply in price, from 205.25p to 217p as the market absorbed the early-morning announcement of the issuance. Only then did they start to fall as expected, ending the day down at 172.59p.

Figure 1.1 - Barclays PLC share price, relative share price and trading volume around 31 October 2008 MCN issue

Source: Thomson Reuters

From publicly issued documents and regulatory news-service releases it is clear that at least one long-short manager that held short positions in Barclays equity bought MCNs in scale (thus covering at least part of their short position at a favourable price), and at least one long-only manager sold existing long positions in ordinary shares and bought a large number of MCNs. Both of these were rational trading strategies. Nevertheless, many millions of arbitrage profits remained available for those able to exploit the opportunity – there was good liquidity in the ordinary shares at prices well above the offered MCN price and there were hours to make the required trades. Why would millions of arbitrage profits be left to collect for hours on end?

If $100 bills were dropped on the sidewalks of Chicago at eight o'clock in the morning, would you expect them to still be there by lunch time?

And yet this appeared to happen on the London Stock Exchange on 31 October 2008.

One possible explanation is that markets were segmented. That is, investors could not buy the MCNs by mandate, or at least were not sure if they could buy the MCNs (and could not get clarification from their compliance and legal teams quickly enough to take advantage of the open offer!).

Another potential explanation is short–selling constraints. About a month earlier, the UK Financial Service Authority had prohibited the active creation or increase of net-short positions in publicly quoted financial companies, although existing short positions were unaffected. This prohibited those traders without legacy short positions in Barclays ordinary shares from under-taking capital-structure arbitrage based around the issue of the MCNs. It is also possible that holders of existing short positions in Barclays' ordinary shares feared that they might have been unable to hold on to these positions until conversion of the MCNs.

Alternatively, they might have been unsure about how many MCNs they could obtain in the open offer (although this seems unlikely – there was a huge supply of MCNs on offer!). Finally, it could simply have been investor error: inertia or a misunderstanding of the nature of the MCNs.

Note from Figure 1.2 below that stock lending did not increase around the time of the MCN issue, consistent with the FSA ban on short-selling (although the increase in stock borrowing in early November is interesting!).

Figure 1.2 - Stock lending activity around 31 October 2008 MCN issue

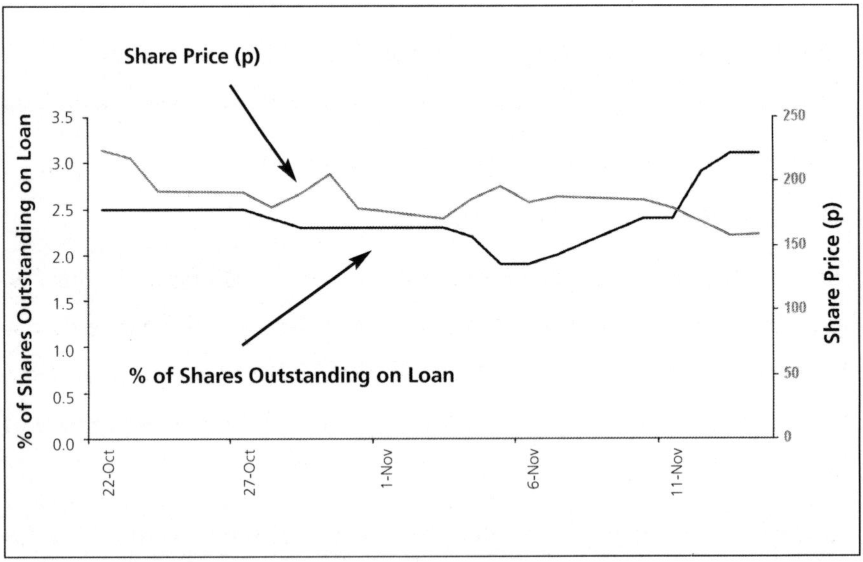

Source: Data Explorers and Thomson Reuters

Two important lessons emerge for traders.

First, they should seek as much trading flexibility as possible (i.e. a broadly-worded mandate).

Secondly, they should approach any new capital instrument as an opportunity for capital-structure arbitrage; immediately reading the prospectus or similar documentation so as to understand the relationships within the new capital structure. Together, these should allow the trader to exploit mis-pricing opportunities that arise as a result of market segmentation.

Short-sale constraints

Earlier, we considered the notion that short-sale constraints matter in markets, as they can prevent traders from exploiting mis-pricings and can lead to security prices remaining over-valued for some time. A short-sale generally requires the borrowing of securities to facilitate the settlement of the transaction[3]. However, it is not always possible to locate securities for borrowing. Also, the short-seller must generally pay a fee to borrow securities, and this can reduce the attractiveness of the short-sale. These problems, plus legal barriers, are known as direct short-sale constraints.

There are also many indirect constraints on short-selling, including the potential for unlimited losses and the risk of being caught in a crowded exit. In extensive interviews that I conducted with short-sellers and prospective short-sellers[4], interviewees identified no less than 34 barriers and difficulties with short-selling. There could even be more than this! These constraints tend to be risk-related, social or institutional in nature.

Perhaps one of the most interesting barriers mentioned is the perception that short-selling is a 'trading' activity rather than an 'investing' activity, so that it becomes unacceptable in the eyes of some stakeholders, such as trustees, consultants and ultimate clients. On the whole, our

---

[3] Naked short-selling and intraday shorting can be exceptions to this rule.

[4] These interviews took place between 2005 and 2009 and involved 31 experienced market practitioners.

> " Interviewees identified no less than 34 barriers and difficulties with short-selling. "

understanding of the risks associated with short-selling is limited. (I examine several of these in greater detail in the next few chapters.)

To what extent do short-sale constraints play a role in limiting arbitrage?

Nagel (2005) argues that institutions are important lenders of stock and that the supply of stock to borrow is likely to be sparser in companies with low institutional ownership. Accordingly, short-sale costs should be higher and constraints more binding in such stocks. Using institutional ownership as a proxy for short-sale constraints, he finds that short-sale constraints help explain apparent return anomalies across stocks, such as "the underperformance of stocks with high market-to-book ratio, analysts' forecast dispersion, turnover or volatility." However, direct short-selling constraints do not fully account for the cross-sectional return differences. Indirect short-sale constraints also matter.

Short-sale constraints can also lead to over-pricing due to the opportunity to speculate that arises when shorting is prohibited. Duffie *et al.* (2002) create a dynamic model of equity prices, stock lending fees and short-interest. They show that a stock price can initially be higher than the greatest valuation of any investor, because the price should include the benefits obtained from being able to lend the stock in future.

A stock price, when limited shorting is permitted, is initially higher than the price with no shorting permitted, as the shareholder expects to earn returns from lending the stock in future. This provides a rebuttal against the common perception that easier access to shorting results in poorer performance for a stock. The authors argue that this can explain the negative stub-value effect associated with some corporate spin-offs (i.e. a negative implied market value for the portion of a parent company not spun off, even though equity is associated with limited liability).

This phenomenon was seen in March 2000 when 3Com sold around 5% of its stake in Palm and the latter went public on the NASDAQ market. 3Com planned to distribute the remainder of its Palm shares directly to existing 3Com shareholders in the ratio of 1.483 Palm shares for each share of 3Com held. An investor wanting to buy a stake in Palm could have bought, say, 1483 shares of Palm or 1000 shares in 3Com. The latter would ultimately have given him 1483 Palm *plus* a share of the assets belonging to 3Com. According to this logic one share of 3Com should have cost at least 1.483 times more than one share of Palm. However on the day of its IPO, Palm shares closed at $95.06 while the shares of 3Com closed at $81.81. This implied a negative stub value for 3Com shares.

In the Duffie *et al.* (2002) model, as lending fees decrease, so too does the valuation associated with the marginal investor and this leads to a decline in stock price. The model also shows that price declines associated with falling lending-fee effects are likely to be greater for companies with a smaller free-float (i.e. a smaller proportion of a company's shares being tradable in public markets) or with larger differences of opinion between investors (as proxied by higher turnover). This is consistent with poor average returns following an initial public offering, when investor opinions are likely to differ greatly (due to low levels of knowledge about the new company) and when free float is likely to be lower (due to lock-ins of stock held by directors and officers).

What next?

In this chapter we have seen that there a variety of reasons for securities prices to diverge from their equilibrium values. In the next chapters, I take a closer look at some of these reasons. In particular, I describe the theory and empirical evidence for each phenomenon, and suggest how traders can avoid mistakes by learning from this evidence. First, I consider predatory trading. This is a form of trading in which well-informed and well-capitalised players exploit weaknesses amongst certain other market players. The notion of predatory trading develops naturally from an ecological view of markets.

As the company approaches a loan covenant (because of, say, an economic downturn) the possibility of it being forced to issue new equity or dispose of assets increases. Predators anticipate such events and can act to exploit their knowledge of the company's loan covenants.

Consider a home-building firm during a housing downturn. As house prices, sales and margins fall, the ratio of the firm's net debt to EBITDA increases and approaches a covenant threshold. The firm (or the lender) could be forced to liquidate inventory (new houses) or undeveloped land amidst the housing downturn – when buyers are scarce and prices achieved are likely to be poor. Other industry players could become aware of this and position themselves accordingly.

Shleifer and Vishny (1992) examine asset sales and describe how liquidity can disappear, imposing costs on the liquidation seller of assets. When financial distress is experienced by several parties within an industry and a liquidation sale takes place, liquidity must come from outsiders who are likely to have lower valuations for the assets and thus bid lower. The authors argue that

> a forced liquidation is often very costly since it is associated with large price impact and low liquidity.

In lieu of asset sales, the distressed firm could be forced by the lending bank(s) to issue new shares to investors. A successful rights issue or placing could bring the net debt to EBITDA and debt-to-equity ratios back into compliance. Traders can anticipate this and short-sell the listed shares of the company, driving the share price lower. The company could ultimately be forced to issue new shares at a time when its share price was trading at a depressed level as a result of the predatory short-selling. Where legally permitted, short-sellers can cover their positions by buying these new shares at the lower issuance price, locking in a profit in the process.

Regulatory limits on financial companies

Similar situations can arise in banks that must maintain minimum capital ratios, and insurance firms that must surpass regulatory solvency thresholds. These ratios can be affected by changes in the value of assets held by the financial institution. During periods of declining asset values, banks and insurers could find themselves approaching these minimum thresholds unless they issue more capital. Opportunities now arise for predators. The predator starts with one or more short positions in financial stocks. Next, by short-selling assets held by banks and insurers, predators could (given sufficient market impact) drive down the price of these assets and thus precipitate breaches of regulatory thresholds. This would induce either forced capital raising or liquidation sales by those companies. The predator now has the opportunity to cover his short positions at a profit.

To counter such a risk, an insurance firm could apply to the regulator for a solvency margin waiver to remove the need for technical, distressed sales; a bank might request the suspension of mark-to-market accounting for some of its assets, or make creative use of the rules governing the classification of assets. For example, re-classifying an asset from the trading book to the 'loans and receivables' category can alleviate the need for mark-to-market accounting of an asset, so long as the asset remains 'unimpaired'.

Predictable behaviour

Any risk management system that requires trading in response to price changes is vulnerable to predation risk. The rigid use of dynamic hedging strategies such as portfolio insurance is one such example. A trader must respond to a price fall by selling part of his holding, until there is no holding left, at which time the selling pressure stops. This trading system is well understood by others in the market and so exposes the user to predation.

The use of stop-loss orders (considered in detail in chapter four) is another example of a risk management system that, rigidly applied, can result in predation. Arguably, risk-management systems should be flexible and somewhat confidential, to reduce the risk of predatory trading. This is not always possible, though, in a society where clarity and transparency of process is often required before one is entrusted with other people's money. Rigidly implemented risk-management systems can have wider unintended consequences for markets, including the creation of liquidity black holes and, in extreme circumstances, crashes[6].

Metallgesellschaft AG

Predictable behaviour in the commodity futures markets also provides opportunities for predators. A famous case involving a change in the structure of oil futures prices and losses from the rolling of futures contracts is the Metallgesellschaft AG (MG) affair of 1993-1994. MG had gone short of oil at long-term, fixed prices in an attempt to build up a new business serving independent gasoline and heating oil marketers. It attempted to hedge this position in the oil futures market, using exchange-traded, near-month futures contracts and rolling them over each month. This imperfect hedge might have worked had the structure of oil futures prices remained favourable. Specifically, MG needed the market to stay in backwardation. With backwardation, the near-term oil futures contract can be sold just before it expires and replaced at a lower price with a more distant oil futures contract.

---

[6] Morris and Shin (2003) show that traders with short decision horizons and limits on their permitted losses can be forced to sell as a response to selling by others, out of fear of breaching their loss limits. This can lead to the creation of so-called 'liquidity black holes', which gather momentum amidst mutually reinforcing sales. The selling is eventually exhausted and the lower security prices attract new buyers, leading to a V-shaped pattern in observed prices.

> " Rigidly implemented risk management systems can have wider unintended consequences for markets, including the creation of liquidity black holes and, in extreme circumstances, crashes. "

However, MG became very large in the market relative to other players, ultimately accounting for about 16% of all the outstanding open interest in NYMEX oil contracts. MG's actions were also predictable. For those traders who were able to anticipate the regular rollover of MG's positions, it was clear that they should short the outgoing contract. The Commitment of Traders reports from this period show that non-commercial traders did indeed take large net short-contract positions, exploiting MG's position.

During 1993, the NYMEX futures market crude-oil contract moved from backwardation to the opposite state, contango. Each futures roll that MG undertook now cost it money. Krapels (2001) described the firm's predicament vividly:

> As long as its huge position was in the market, MG hung there like a big *piñata* inviting others to hit it each month.

MG had made the error of becoming predictable in its behaviour and large enough to be noticed. It had also mistakenly assumed that backwardation was the normal condition of oil markets. MG's mark-to-market losses in its long-futures position increased and it was unable to meet margin calls from NYMEX. MG ultimately terminated its strategy and closed its positions at a large loss.

Futures roll-overs

Studies into the long-term returns obtained from commodity futures suggest that roll-returns have made up an important part of total return, lack of liquid assets which can be sold to raise cash), he would be forced to liquidate some of his positions. This situation could become known to others parties, including those involved in financing the trades and even their broader social circle. The leveraged trader is now at risk from predatory trading.

If predators do indeed attack his positions, losses arising from the liquidation sale would become exaggerated. In an alternative scenario, the trader need not even have suffered any initial losses on his positions. If a prime broker spontaneously increases the margin requirements for positions, a trader could be faced with an unexpected margin call that he is unable to meet. This too could result in a need to liquidate and the risk of predatory trading against him. Tightened credit terms and an inability to meet margin calls are believed to have been behind the well-publicised liquidation of Peloton Partners' $2 billion ABS Fund in 2008.

Even traders who have yet to breach margin requirements can attract predators. Simply *approaching* a margin call threshold can become problematic, as knowledgeable predators start to trade in anticipation of a future liquidation. This anticipatory trading can *precipitate* financial distress.

Loan covenants

As another illustration, banks that lend money to companies often place covenants on those loans. For example, a bank may set an upper limit on the ratio of the borrowing firm's debt-to-equity ratio, or the firm's net debt to EBITDA[5] ratio. Where a firm breaches a loan covenant, the bank gains the power to seize assets or to demand actions from management that brings the ratios back into compliance with the covenants.

---

[5] EBITDA: earnings before interest, tax, depreciation and amortisation. A measure of income.

Predatory trading involves the exploitation of knowledge about the strategies and positions of other market participants. In particular, when a trader learns about another large player's *need* to trade, an opportunity could arise to profit from the situation. The predator trades in such a way as to benefit from the market impact of forced transactions by the prey.

Predatory trading relies on the assumption that large trades that demand liquidity from the market can move market prices. A trade will have market impact whenever its scale and immediacy exceeds the market's ability to absorb it.

There are many reasons why a market participant might be forced to trade. One of the simplest of these is financial distress. Where a borrower runs into financial difficulties, this can result in a liquidation sale of the borrower's assets at the behest of the lender. If the asset sales are large enough, they can have market impact. Knowing that a trader is in financial distress and that liquidation is imminent or underway, a predator initially trades in the same direction as the prey. This has the effect of withdrawing liquidity from the market. As a result, the market impact of the liquidation becomes greater than might otherwise be expected. The security price fall resulting from the liquidation becomes exaggerated, imposing losses on the prey. The predator then reverses his trading direction, exploiting the price over-shooting and closing out his position at a profit.

Margin call

As an illustration, take the case of a leveraged long-short trader who finds that some of his trades have become unprofitable. As a result of the short-term losses, he receives a margin call from his prime-broker. If unable to meet that margin call (say, because of limited capital and a

CHAPTER 2

PREDATORY TRADING

helping commodity-futures returns to appear attractive relative to those of some other asset classes. Furthermore, these returns have not been fully correlated to those of other asset classes. Perhaps based on these studies a popular strategy amongst diversified investors has been to seek some exposure to commodity markets via baskets of commodity futures. Many exchange-traded funds, such as the US Oil Fund LP (ticker: USO), facilitate this demand. Funds such as this roll billions of dollars of assets from oil futures approaching expiry to those contracts with more distant expiry. This large-scale and predictable trading activity provides exploitable opportunities for predators. By pre-positioning ahead of the roll date, a predator can benefit from the market impact of the ETF.

Insofar as this predation takes place, one might expect a change in conditions in each futures market, from backwardation towards contango in advance of the scheduled roll dates of large ETFs. Roll returns could become negative and the total returns achieved by holders of the ETF would suffer. Such a pattern would be likely to continue for as long as these funds remain significant players in futures markets and trade in a predictable manner; or until regulations disallow the front-running of their trades.

Open-ended funds

Another popular predatory trading strategy is the short-selling of securities that are believed to be held by open-ended funds experiencing client redemptions.

Where an open-ended fund, such as a mutual fund, has performed poorly, clients are prone to redeem units, perhaps believing that the trend of losses will continue. Large-scale client redemptions generate a need for cash (except in special cases where redemptions can be

> **By pre-positioning ahead of the roll date, a predator can benefit from the market impact of the ETF.**

suspended or where an *in specie* transfer is permitted in lieu of cash redemption payments). The need for cash leads the fund manager to sell securities held by the fund. Where the fund's holding are known to the outside world, mass client redemptions can lead to predictable, forced trading of known securities and the opportunity for predators to earn profits.

A trader's ability to predict which funds will be forced to transact gives rise to an incentive for predatory trading. In an interview with the *Financial Times* (6 June, 2005), Jonathan Bailey, a founding partner of Bailey Coates Asset Management, a London-based hedge-fund manager, suggested that other hedge funds and investment bank proprietary trading desks had "attacked his company's portfolio on rumours of redemptions from the fund". He added, "there has been speculative short selling against our positions – that is fact." Clearly, this trader believed that he had become a victim of predatory trading.

Fire sales

Coval and Stafford (2007) studied such asset "fire sales" in equity markets – forced, immediate sales for which counter-parties can demand large liquidity premia. They found "considerable support for the notion that widespread selling by financially distressed mutual funds leads to fire-sale prices". They also examined large inflows to funds and found that managers behaved as if constrained to quickly add to existing positions, resulting in persistent upward price pressure on these securities. The price effects from these sets of actions are long-lasting and the fire sale effect increases with the number of sellers and the level of financial distress.

Even funds initially unaffected by financial distress can later become distressed: selling by distressed funds of commonly held securities hurts the performance of other funds, leading to investors' redemptions and subsequent distress in those funds. Where the securities have poor liquidity (e.g. micro cap stocks or complex structured products) the effects will be most pronounced. The authors argue:

> the asset fire sale story provides a mechanism for rational mis-pricing. The market is clearly somewhat inefficient, in that market prices are not perfectly reflective of all available information. However, the basis of this mis-pricing requires neither irrational investors nor managers. Prices eventually reflect available information, but sometimes with a significant delay.

In other words, market prices can diverge from equilibrium value for good reason, and these mis-pricings can persist for quite some time. This is where strategic traders earn their profits.

The injection of external capital into a distressed fund (or into the book of a distressed trader) is one way of alleviating the problem of forced liquidation. This is generally difficult to achieve, though – external capital would be needed just at a time when performance had been poor.

Nevertheless, there have been some high-profile examples of distressed funds receiving external capital just in time to prevent large-scale liquidations. These include the injection of $3 billion of capital into Goldman Sachs Asset Management's Global Equity Opportunities fund in August 2007. This equity long/short quant fund suffered large

" Market prices can diverge from equilibrium value for good reason, and these mis-pricings can persist for quite some time. "

losses as a result of what the firm called "market dislocation impacting equity quantitative strategies". Rather than being forced to liquidate losing positions, the injection of outside capital allowed the fund to retain positions that appeared to offer attractive expected returns.

The perfect predator

In general terms, predatory trading is suited to traders who can take both long and short positions, and who are relatively unconstrained by benchmarks or risk management systems. Predatory trading is most profitable in markets with poor liquidity and in situations where a forced trader's position is large relative to the capacity of predators. The perfect predator would be flexible (able to operate across many markets, including those with poor liquidity), strong (i.e. well-capitalised compared to the prey) and knowledgeable about the ecology of the markets (i.e. about the capital, positions and strategies of others).

Brunnermeier and Pedersen model

A number of academic papers have built models to examine predatory trading and its implications for markets. For example, Brunnermeier and Pedersen (2005) built a model containing two assets: a riskless bond and a risky asset. There are two kinds of agents in their market eco-system: large strategic traders (akin to hedge funds and proprietary traders) and long-term investors (akin to pension funds and individual investors). Long-term investors are price takers and demand more of the risky asset when its price is lower. Strategic traders are risk neutral and seek to maximise their wealth; their trades have market impact and so they moderate their trading intensity to minimise price impact costs. A price shock can lead to financial distress in a strategic trader, and this can result in a need to liquidate holdings in the risky asset. Such liquidations create opportunities for other strategic traders to exploit.

Predatory trading in the Brunnermeier and Pedersen model drives prices *away* from intrinsic value. It also drains liquidity from the market, as predatory traders and the liquidator each trade in the same direction, making the market one-sided.

The authors argue that there are three ways to value large positions in the risky asset:

1. the current market price,

2. the orderly liquidation value which is generally lower, and finally

3. the distressed liquidation value, which is lower still.

Selling by a predator leads to an exaggerated decline in the price of a security that is being liquidated. Liquidation is very costly for the prey, as he would sell around the distressed liquidation value. A predator benefits from the market impact of these forced transactions. He makes money by selling assets early and buying them back around the distressed liquidation value; and by buying additional assets cheaply until he reaches his capacity.

The following chart illustrates the typical price action in a risky asset that is subject to liquidation by a distressed agent and to predatory trading. The price declines dramatically from its starting price of 150 due to the market impact of the liquidating agent and the predator(s) selling their assets. As the liquidation ends (time 0), the predator(s) buy back their stock (and could potentially buy more). Their market impact boosts the asset price until a new equilibrium price is reached (130 in this example).

Figure 2.1 - Price over time for a risky asset subject to liquidation and predatory trading

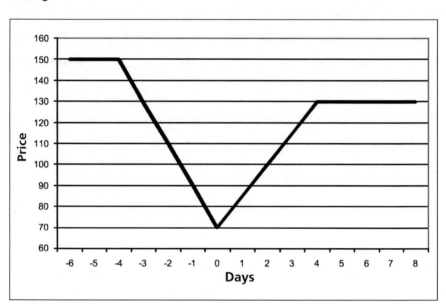

When a liquidation occurs, predatory traders have an incentive to destabilise prices (i.e. move them away from recent equilibrium levels).

Short sellers

Shkilko *et al.* (2008) examine all trades and quotes on NASDAQ from May 2005 to May 2006 to study

> a relatively unexplored class of short-sellers; the class that, instead of enhancing market efficiency, occasionally manipulates prices.

They show that short-sellers substantially increase their activity following significant negative-order imbalances created by non-short trades, contributing to price overshooting. Thus, intraday liquidity crises are exacerbated by short-sellers. Their results provide empirical support for the predictions of Brunnermeier and Pedersen's theoretical model of predatory trading.

SOES

In related research, Bentson and Wood (2006) investigate trading strategies associated with the small-order execution service (SOES) on NASDAQ. They examine the period during which market makers were obliged to instantly honour trades placed through SOES at quoted prices for up to 1000 shares, with up to five repetitions. Traders used this right to pursue a variety of trading strategies, one of which involved a form of predatory trading. According to the authors, traders attempt to:

> identify the onset of buy/sell programs by institutional investors, stepping in front of these programs by absorbing the available liquidity, and then resupplying the liquidity at short-term profit.

This technique exploits the desire or need of institutions to trade large positions in securities that have limited liquidity.

LTCM

A case study into predatory trading is provided by Cai (2003) who used a detailed audit trail of transactions around the time of the Long-Term Capital Management (LTCM) crisis of 1998, to investigate if market makers in the CBOT Treasury bond futures market, who may have had superior knowledge about customer order flow, exploited their information advantage to trade to the detriment of LTCM when the firm faced binding margin constraints. She found evidence of market makers systematically front running, by two to three minutes, the trades of one entity around the time of the crisis.

Credit downgrades

Another opportunity for predatory traders arises in bonds subject to credit rating downgrades. Investors in bonds that are subject to a downgrade may be forced to sell (by mandate or even by legal requirements) if the rating falls below investment grade and into junk bond status. Such rules are primarily designed to reduce portfolio risk – in this case the risk of holding bonds with heightened credit risk. However, the imposition of a rigid rule creates a new risk – predation risk.

There now follow price charts for bonds issued by the Royal Bank of Scotland and ABN AMRO, around the time of their credit rating downgrades to junk status in January 2009. A credit rating downgrade reflects the rating agency's recognition of higher default risk (i.e. a deterioration in fundamentals). It also presents an opportunity for predators to exploit other bond holders' requirement to sell, regardless of price. The price chart shows a similar pattern to the theoretical movement in prices expected where predatory trading occurs. The price eventually settles at a much lower level than suggested by the theoretical chart, presumably because the credit-rating downgrade brought new information to the market about default risk.

Figure 2.2 - RBS downgraded to BB by S&P on 19 January 2009

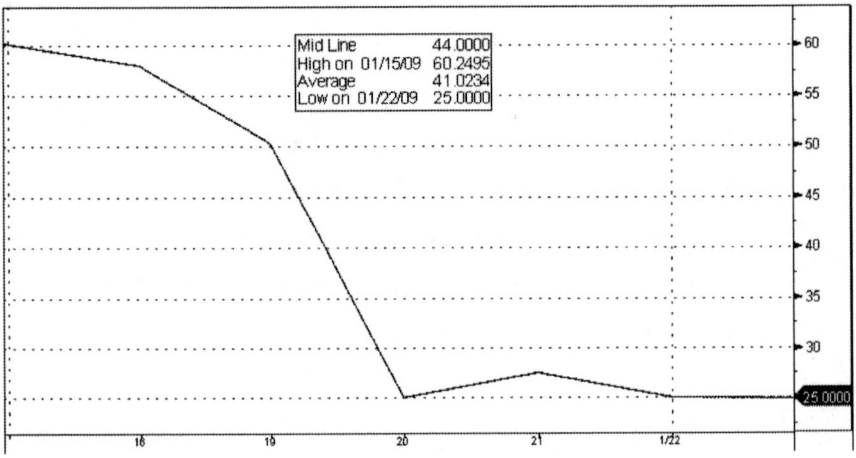

Source: Bloomberg

Figure 2.3 - ABN AMRO downgraded to BB+ by S&P on 20 January 2009

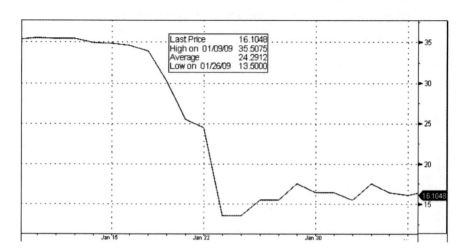

Last Price	16.1048
High on 01/09/09	35.5075
Average	24.2912
Low on 01/26/09	13.5000

Source: Bloomberg

Multiple predators, multiple prey

When multiple predators are involved, each predator should attempt to front run the liquidating agent as before, but should now seek to buy back his risky assets before the other predators. This leads the game to move forward to some extent, so that predators are buying back assets before the distressed agent has completed his liquidation.

This new dynamic in the market ecology means that the price exaggeration from predatory trading is *less* pronounced and the cost associated with liquidation is lower. If all the predatory traders were able to collude and thus co-ordinate their actions, they could jointly act like a single predator. This would result in greater price overshooting.

With multiple prey, the dynamics are quite different. A crisis in a financially distressed trader can spill over to other traders and markets. When several traders are in financial distress, it becomes harder for the un-distressed traders to survive. There are more asset sales and fewer competing predators and so the price fall becomes more exaggerated. This leads to the risk of the distressed potentially bringing down a number of otherwise non-distressed agents with them. As traders facing the need to liquidate increase in number, defaults occur and a ripple-effect is created.

This contagion creates systemic risk in the market and attracts the attention of regulators, who seek to reduce such risks. Regulatory interventions or bailouts can reduce such systemic risks, but limit the opportunities for strong predators.

Predatory trading and stock price manipulation

The Brunnermeier and Pedersen model is constructed in such a way that a trader cannot make money as a result of his own trades. Instead, a trader can only make money by exploiting the way other traders affect prices. Thus, the model attempts to distinguish predatory trading from (illegal) price manipulation. The authors argue that

> a distinctive feature of predatory behaviour [as distinct from market manipulation] is that one benefits from the market impact of the prey, not from one's own market impact.

It should be noted, though, that trading in advance of an anticipated trade *induces* the anticipated trade. For example, short-selling a stock held by a mutual fund facing client redemptions helps drive down the stock's price, hurting the fund's performance and making future redemptions more likely. As such, predatory trading and stock price manipulation share some characteristics. This calls into question the ethics and legality of predatory trading.

In an article entitled 'Arbitraging Arbitrageurs', Attari *et al.* (2005) build a model with one risky asset and three types of agents: an arbitrageur, a strategic trader and a large number of small liquidity traders. The arbitrageur practises statistical arbitrage, or model-driven convergence trading, and the strategic trader attempts to benefit from knowledge of the arbitrageur's financial condition.

Strategic trader vs the arbs

When the arbitrageur is well-capitalised, the strategic trader finds it best to be inactive. When advantageous, the strategic trader can lend money to the arbitrageur, much as a prime broker might do. However, as the financial position of the arbitrageur weakens, the strategic trader starts to trade. Specifically, he engages in predatory trading against the arbitrageur.

As the arbitrageur approaches financial distress, he will attempt to remain solvent by supporting the price of the asset (i.e. the arbitrageur is modelled to be an unethical price manipulator!). For a financially fragile arbitrageur:

> the trades of the sophisticated traders can be detrimental enough
> to tip the balance against recovery of the arbitrageur, forcing him
> into insolvency.

Upon insolvency, the arbitrageur liquidates his assets and the strategic trader buys, thus providing liquidity to the market.

The authors show that strategic traders can use their knowledge of the financial state of an arbitrageur to "benefit from the predictable price deviations caused by a financially constrained arbitrageur's trades." In other words, this theoretical model shows that prime brokers possess knowledge that can be abused to predate their clients.

A closer look at index-fund predation

Index-fund predation is perhaps the best known form of predatory trading. It involves trading ahead of full-replication index funds as they

> " This theoretical model shows that prime brokers possess knowledge that can be abused to predate their clients. "

periodically rebalance their portfolios in response to changes in index constituents.

Any market participant operating in a predictable and transparent fashion can expect to attract the attention of predators. Where the predictable trades involve highly liquid securities and are small in scale, there will be little market impact and a low risk of predatory activity. However, where an investment strategy experiences success, assets devoted to that strategy are likely to grow, through a combination of organic growth and new money in-flows. As assets grow, the market impact of the strategy grows and predators will be increasingly attracted by opportunities to benefit from this market impact.

Where predatory trading becomes profitable, the strategy's performance suffers. This pattern applies equally to full-replication index funds: strong performance relative to the average active fund combined with low fees and good diversification eventually attracts more assets to the strategy. Increasing market impact creates greater opportunities for predators but economic losses for index-fund clients. This suggests a constraint on the proportion of full-replication index funds we should expect to find within a market ecosystem.

US evidence

In a study of the losses that index funds face at the hands of arbitrageurs, Chen *et el.* (2006) show that funds linked to the S&P 500 index and the Russell 2000 index lose between $1 billion and $2.1 billion each year because of front-running by index-fund predators who are aware of the tracking error constraints placed on index funds. They thus show that predatory trading is economically important.

Predatory trading also affects the *long-term* returns achieved by index funds. Siegel and Schwartz (2006) compared the long-term returns from the original 1957 S&P 500 companies to returns from the S&P 500 index (with all its rebalances) to the end of 2003. They created portfolios that accounted for spin-offs, mergers etc, so as to avoid survivor bias[7]. Portfolios created from the original S&P 500 constituents and their descendants outperformed the S&P 500 index over the period studied, and with

> " Funds linked to the S&P 500 index and the Russell 2000 index lose between $1 billion and $2.1 billion each year because of front-running by index-fund predators. "

lower volatility of returns. Amongst the possible reasons they gave for this phenomenon was index-fund predation.

S&P 500 index reviews

Stock returns around the announcement of index additions and deletions have been examined extensively in the United States. The most widely tracked US index is the Standard and Poor's 500 (S&P 500) and most studies have been directed towards this popular benchmark. The constituents of the S&P 500 index are determined by the Standard and Poor's Index Committee. Since October 1989, Standard and Poor's has announced changes in S&P 500 constituents one week in advance of

---

[7] Survivor bias occurs when a study reflects only the results from firms that survived throughout the period of study, ignoring those that existed during only part of the study. Firms that disappeared part way through the study might have produced different returns from those that survived.

implementation of these changes[8]. Additions to the S&P 500 are only made when stocks must be removed. Reasons for removal include a merger or acquisition, restructuring, bankruptcy, or when a company no longer meets the criteria for inclusion in the index. To identify replacements, the Committee selects from pre-approved companies in its secret candidate-replacement pool. This pool contains companies that represent important or emerging US industries, are large within their industries, and have widely held shares, high trading volume and financial soundness.

On average, stocks added to the S&P 500 index experience positive abnormal returns from the day of the announcement through to the day before implementation (or through to the close of implementation day, depending on the study) with a partial reversal thereafter. For deletions, the pattern of stock returns is similar, but in the opposite direction.

For example, Beneish and Whaley (1997) report positive abnormal returns of 6% for companies added to S&P 500 from October 1989 through December 1995, from the close of trading on the announcement day until the close of trading on the implementation day. Lynch and Mendenhall (1997) argue that the price reversal on and after the implementation date indicates that heavy trading around the time of the index change causes stock prices to move temporarily away from their equilibrium values. Some researchers argue that becoming a major index constituent leads to increased trading volume and greater attention from analysts, reducing bid-ask spreads and improving liquidity. This could explain the positive abnormal returns observed in

---

[8] There have been a few exceptions to this, including a 16-day implementation period for Microsoft's admittance in 1994, in order to cope with its large scale, and a one-day implementation for the Prime Motors Inn deletion in 1990 due to its bankruptcy filing (source: Beneish and Whaley, 1996).

promoted stocks after the announcement day. However, it would not explain the reversals subsequent to implementation.

A Standard and Poor's study (Blitzer and Dash, 2004) shows that abnormal returns associated with index announcements have been falling in the period from 1998 to 2004. This pattern applies to S&P 500, S&P MidCap 400 and S&P Small Cap 600 index additions. They argue that these diminished abnormal returns are not due to falls in excess trading volume around the time of index changes, nor are they due to reduced demand from index funds or an increase in inter-index moves. Instead, they suggest that increased risk-arbitrage activity around index changes has boosted competition and lowered returns. Also, some index funds now trade in a more flexible manner around the implementation date, and an increase in assets in mid and small-cap indices reduces net demand, due to an offset effect between indices. They argue that such changes in the index effect over time need to be factored into the development of trading strategies.

The UK is different

Much less work has been done on examining UK index funds and index changes. And yet, because of a different institutional framework, the UK FTSE indices are arguably better suited to predatory trading than the S&P 500 index. This is because of greater transparency in the index rebalancing process, which leads to greater opportunities to successfully anticipate index changes.

Analysis of FTSE 350 Index

Consider, for example, the FTSE 350 index. The organisation and management of this index is undertaken by the FTSE Europe/Middle East/Africa Regional Committee. The Committee meets quarterly to review the constituents of the FTSE 350. Since April 1992, the meetings to review the constituents are held on the Wednesday after the first Friday in March, June, September and December. The day on which the Committee meets is known as the review day. Any constituent changes are implemented on the trading day following the expiry of the LIFFE futures and options contracts, which normally takes place on the third Friday of the same month.[9] This is known as the implementation day. There is a consistent number of trading days between the review and implementation dates (six trading days).

Inclusion in the FTSE 350 Index is based on published rules that are concerned with a stock's free float market capitalisation and liquidity. These rules are clearly described by the FTSE Policy Group and so market participants interested in the outcome of the quarterly review (e.g. index trackers or active mangers with trading strategies based around index revisions) should be in a position to make relatively accurate predictions of the changes shortly before the announcement.

There now follows the results of a study that examined whether companies added/deleted from the FTSE 100 and FTSE 350 index earn statistically significant abnormal returns around the review and implementation period.[10]

Data were collected from Datastream for the four-year period from June 2001 to September 2005, during which time there were 214 additions and 202 deletions (see Table 2.1). Differences between the number of additions and deletions can arise because of the effect of merger, acquisition and spin-off activity, and because in some instances the FTSE 350 index comprises more than 350 companies.

---

[9] Ground Rules for the Management of the UK Series, V10.5 May 2008, Rule 6.1.1.

[10] This work was undertaken in 2005 in conjunction with Dr Charalambos Constantinou. Financial support was kindly provided by Aberdeen Asset Management.

Table 2.1 - Summary statistics for additions/deletions to FTSE 350 Index

Review Month	Additions	Deletions
Jun-01	16	16
Sep-01	23	23
Dec-01	10	10
Mar-02	7	7
Jun-02	13	11
Sep-02	15	15
Dec-02	17	16
Mar-03	7	7
Jun-03	12	12
Sep-03	13	11
Dec-03	11	10
Mar-04	9	7
Jun-04	12	10
Sep-04	8	7
Dec-04	6	6
Mar-05	10	9
Jun-05	12	12
Sep-05	13	13

In order to examine the impact of additions and deletions on stock returns, I adopted a standard event-study methodology, calculating daily risk-adjusted, or abnormal, returns for each company that is added to, or deleted from, the index. I made these calculations from 30-days before the index review meeting, up to 30-days afterwards. There is an ongoing debate about how best to measure risk in equity returns, and thus how to calculate risk-adjusted or abnormal returns. In this study I use the market model, which is widely used for this kind of short-term analysis [see the appendices for full descriptions].

For the period studied, companies added to the FTSE 350 Index significantly out-performed the FTSE 350 index ahead of the revision day. On an average cumulative basis, these companies out-performed the index by 5.6% for a 30-days holding period before the review day. For the 30-day period following the review day, an equally-weighted portfolio of companies added to the index significantly under-performed the benchmark index by 6.5%. Figure 2.4 shows the average cumulative abnormal returns for these periods around the review day (which is shown as day 0).

Figure 2.4 - Cumulative abnormal returns around the revision and implementation dates of additions to the FTSE 350 Index

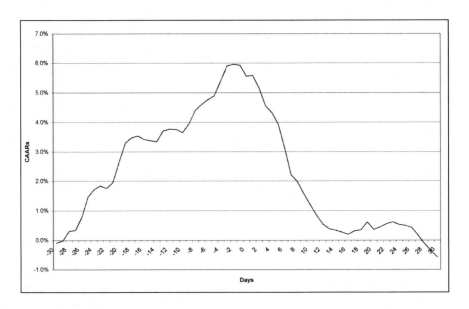

Next, I consider companies that were deleted from the FTSE 350 Index. Cumulative abnormal returns for an equally-weighted portfolio of the deleted companies for the 30-day period before index deletion were significantly negative (-4.9%). For the 30-days after the review day, abnormal returns were positive, but statistically insignificant. Figure 2.5 shows the cumulative abnormal returns around the review day for deleted stocks. A partial reversion in cumulative abnormal returns after the review day is apparent, but is not statistically significant.

Figure 2.5 - Cumulative abnormal returns around the revision and implementation dates of deletions to the FTSE 350 Index

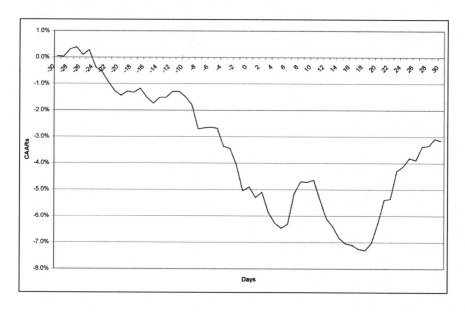

The following table provides details of the average abnormal returns on key dates, and cumulative average abnormal returns for various time periods.

Table 2.2 - Price effects around the revision date and implementation dates for additions to (and deletions from) the FTSE 350 Index

Panel A. Average Abnormal Returns (AARs)					
Additions			**Deletions**		
Day	**AARs (%)**	**P-value***	**Day**	**AARs (%)**	**P-value***
-15	-0.04	0.21	-15	-0.22	0.12
-14	-0.03	0.98	-14	0.22	0.14
-13	0.36	0.02†	-13	0.01	0.70
-12	0.06	0.52	-12	0.22	0.64
-10	-0.01	0.65	-10	0.01	0.82
-11	-0.11	0.98	-11	-0.20	0.42
-9	0.30	0.01‡	-9	-0.30	0.30
-8	0.45	0.07*	-8	-0.91	0.02†
-7	0.20	0.16	-7	0.04	0.75
-6	0.17	0.85	-6	0.02	0.90
-5	0.13	0.35	-5	-0.03	0.58
-4	0.50	0.00‡	-4	-0.70	0.00‡
-3	0.51	0.12	-3	-0.07	0.33
-2	0.06	0.70	-2	-0.62	0.00‡
-1	-0.03	0.93	-1	-0.97	0.00‡
Revision Day	**-0.37**	**0.00‡**	**Revision Day**	**0.14**	**0.78**
1	0.02	0.58	1	-0.40	0.36
2	-0.42	0.03†	2	0.20	0.64
3	-0.61	0.00‡	3	-0.77	0.00‡
4	-0.23	0.82	4	-0.41	0.16
5	-0.39	0.05†	5	-0.18	0.85
6	-0.81	0.00‡	6	0.15	0.52
7	-0.91	0.00‡	7	1.16	0.00‡
Implem. Day	**-0.24**	**0.02†**	**Implem. Day**	**0.45**	**0.14**
9	-0.40	0.05†	9	-0.02	0.97
10	-0.37	0.11	10	0.08	0.91
11	-0.36	0.04†	11	-0.75	0.00‡
12	-0.30	0.07*	12	-0.71	0.02†
13	-0.16	0.06*	13	-0.30	0.38
14	-0.05	0.62	14	-0.43	0.12
15	-0.07	0.72	15	-0.21	0.38

Panel B. Cumulative Average Abnormal Returns (CAARs)					
Window Period	CAARs (%)	P-value*	Window Period	CAARs (%)	P-value*
(-30,-0)	5.6	0.00‡	(-30,-0)	-4.9	0.00‡
(-20,-0)	3.6	0.00‡	(-20,-0)	-3.6	0.00‡
(-10,0)	1.8	0.01‡	(-10,0)	-3.6	0.00‡
(-1,0)	-0.4	0.05†	(-1,0)	-0.8	0.00‡
(-1,1)	-0.4	0.11	(-1,1)	-1.2	0.00‡
(0,1)	-0.3	0.03†	(0,1)	-0.3	0.66
(0,10)	-4.7	0.00‡	(0,10)	0.4	0.76
(0,20)	-5.6	0.00‡	(0,20)	-1.2	0.32
(0,30)	-6.5	0.00‡	(0,30)	1.9	0.66

‡, †, and * denotes significance at the 1, 5 and 10 level of significance respectively.

In summary:

- companies **added** to the FTSE 350 Index earned *positive* abnormal returns for a holding period of 30 days before the review day, with a full reversal thereafter;
- companies **deleted** from the index earned *negative* abnormal returns for a holding period of 30 days before the review day, with a statistically insignificant partial reversal thereafter.

I also conducted separate tests on the FTSE 100 Index. The patterns observed were weaker, but still statistically significant.

The results for FTSE indices show a different dynamic from that associated with the S&P 500 Index. This is probably the consequence of using different processes (and different degrees of transparency) in the selection and rebalancing of index constituents.

Evidence from studies such as this provides a basis upon which predators can develop trading strategies. It should also provide valuable information for index-fund managers, potentially encouraging them to develop flexible approaches to index-fund management.

Index managers without any flexibility are likely to achieve low tracking error against an index, but should expect (absolute) returns to be eroded by predatory trading. The key point here is that there is a trade-off between low tracking error and higher returns. As a result of predatory trading, inflexible index funds can overpay for stocks that are promoted to an index, and receive poor price for stocks that are deleted from the index. The index return is not the same as the market return.

Index funds evolve…

A number of full replication index funds are aware of the potential losses at the hands of predators and have evolved, developing alternative strategies in an attempt to reduce losses. The academic literature provides some clues as to these alternative strategies.

For example, Chen *et al.* (2006) suggest that the losses to index funds can be reduced by:

- relaxing the tracking error constraints

- developing 'silent indices'

- using rarely-used indices in an ever-changing fashion

- using index-rebalancing methodologies that are less predictable, less transparent or less frequent.

By relaxing tracking error constraints and using an alternative approach to full replication (such as stratified sampling or optimisation[11]), an index-fund manager is no longer forced to trade in every security added to, or deleted from, an index (although there will be pressure to trade

---

[11] Stratified sampling is a method of sampling from a population that involves grouping members of the population into somewhat homogenous sub-groups before sampling. In an index fund, this might involve grouping stocks by sector and then sampling within sectors, so as to match sector weights exactly. Optimisation approaches can use techniques such as quadratic programming or genetic algorithms to optimise, say, tracking error with respect to trading costs.

in most of these). Flexibility can also be obtained by allowing for trading in shares or equivalent derivative products on days other than implementation day.

> **❝ Index return is not the same as the market return. ❞**

Within the UK context, this might even include trading ahead of the review day, where a revision is known with some certainty. As a result, the predatory trading game moves forward, possibly even ahead of the review day. Predatory traders would aim to win this game by guessing correctly and guessing early. They would need to take account of the actions of other active traders playing the same game. Where there are many predators, the closing of positions begins before the index fund manager is expected to make his trades. Index funds with high flexibility can also move early, but need to be more cognisant of tracking error. The patterns of cumulative average abnormal returns found in my UK study suggest that the index-fund predation game is well developed.

Active managers, in placing their bets on likely promotions to, and deletions from, the index constituent list, can influence share prices through their market impact. One or more active managers, trading in scale and with sufficient market impact, can, in a sense, make the index changes happen, by moving the share price and hence the market capitalisation of a firm to a level that ensures its promotion or deletion from the index.

Through this process, predators' actions can change prices and influence index composition. This in turn affects demand for a company's shares and thus influences its share price. This phenomenon is akin to the notion of reflexivity espoused by George Soros[12].

---

[12] Reflexivity in a market setting asserts that security prices can affect fundamentals. Changes in fundamentals can proceed to affect expectations and, in turn, prices. This can become a self-reinforcing pattern.

Could anticipatory trading that influences index composition be construed as market manipulation?

It would be very difficult for an observer to differentiate between trades representing a genuine attempt to guess at likely index revisions, and those intended to manipulate the market.

Risks in anticipating index revisions

Anticipating index revisions can be a risky game. The risk takes two forms.

Revision risk

First, there is 'revision risk' – the risk of incorrectly guessing at revision candidates. Even with clearly described rules determining the constituents of an index, it will not be possible to evaluate exactly which shares will be added or deleted from the index. A company's share price, and thus market capitalisation, will be 'noisy'. Furthermore, a surge in general market confidence, say, is likely to affect more volatile, or higher-beta, stocks most favourably. This could lead to an unexpected candidate being promoted at the expense of some previously more-favoured candidate. As market capitalisations rise and fall ahead of review day, so there is a risk that a candidate company does not 'make the cut' for index addition or deletion.

Fundamental risk

Secondly, there is 'fundamental risk' – a company may be added or deleted as expected, but could suffer a change in fundamentals during the period just before index-review day. This could take the form of either company specific news, or general news that affects candidate shares to a greater or lesser relative extent. As an illustration, a company with a high likelihood of index promotion could announce weaker than anticipated corporate results just ahead of the review day. It might still get promoted to the index; but for predators holding the stock, the share price fall following the poor corporate results could out-weigh any benefit arising from promotion to the index.

As an example of this phenomenon, consider PartyGaming Plc in September 2005: the company was almost certain to enter the FTSE 100 index that month and predators were likely to have built up anticipatory positions. However, after announcing poorer than expected growth prospects on 6 September, the firm's shares fell by 33% in one day. The company did indeed enter the FTSE 100 index that month, but those who bought before 6 September in anticipation of FTSE 100 entry suffered as a result of the deterioration in fundamentals.

To understand fully the risks and potential returns from index-fund predation, it is necessary to examine the returns from stock that *might* have been added to, or ejected from, the index, but were not. The predator could have been trading in these stocks and is likely to have experienced a very different distribution of returns from these stocks than from those that were indeed promoted to, or ejected from, the index.

Provisional research shows that stocks that surprise by failing to get promoted perform badly on average for some period of time after the disappointment. The performance of predators will depend on the trading rules adopted and patterns are likely to vary over time as the market ecology develops. There will also be trading costs, including commissions, stamp duty where applicable, bid-offer spreads and market impact to consider. Only then will it be possible to determine if consistently profitable rule-based trading strategies can be formed.

In practice, a successful predator is likely to supplement specific trading rules with experience and judgement, to weigh possible returns against revision risk and fundamental risk prior to the revision date.

Conditions that suit index-fund predation

Index-fund predation is likely to be most successful when the index rebalancing process is transparent and known in advance; when there are few predators; when a particular index is heavily used by index funds; when liquidity in the securities is poor; and when index-fund managers have little flexibility in their approach.

Unsurprisingly, predation risk can be particularly acute for equity indices containing smaller companies. Illiquidity in small-cap stocks requires paying significant price concessions for executing large trades in short time periods. This can lead to performance shortfalls against a benchmark. Keim (1999) argues that

> it is the responsibility of passive fund managers to adopt investment rules and procedures that reduce these trade costs.

For small-cap index-fund managers, this is likely to include deviations from the underlying index.

Dimensional Fund Advisors (DFA) 9-10 Fund

A well-documented example is the Dimensional Fund Advisors (DFA) 9-10 Fund, a micro-cap (smallest two deciles of market capitalisation) US equity fund, which allows for deviations in portfolio holdings from the index so as to minimise trading costs. The fund is allowed to hold (with some limitations) stocks that have grown too large for the micro-cap index to help control trading costs, so that the fund is never a forced-seller whose future actions are known with certainty by the market.

The fund can also make use of a 'redemption in kind' feature. During falling markets, large-scale client redemptions from an open-ended mutual fund generally lead the manager to sell holdings, so as to raise the cash needed to meet the client redemptions. This can develop into a vicious circle – selling by the manager to meet redemptions forces the price of the securities to fall. Where the fund still has holdings in these securities, price drops lead to falls in the net asset value (NAV) per share in the fund. Falling NAVs can prompt further client redemptions, and so on, in a form of death spiral. Having resort to a redemption-in-kind facility allows the manager to offer not cash but securities (in this case, illiquid micro-cap securities) to the client. This makes redemption during such a situation unattractive to the client, and might help to prevent a death spiral of this form.

In summary, index funds are considered by many to be ideal vehicles for long-term investment, and studies suggest that the average *active* fund under-performs an index fund after fees and expenses are considered. And yet, index funds are vulnerable to predatory trading as a result of their predictable behaviour. The empirical evidence shows that predators impose economically significant losses on index funds.

Some index funds have adapted to hostile environments and developed new strategies to reduce the risk of attack from predators. Of course, the predators can respond to the mutations of those index funds, and so on. This would lead us to expect an ever changing cycle of market activity, much like that described by Niederhoffer.

The ethics of predatory trading

As research and knowledge of predatory trading grows, it is also important to understand the legality and ethics of the practice. Predatory trading represents an immature area of financial law and ethics. To investigate this issue, I examine legal and regulatory pronouncements and the literature on financial ethics. I also interview a number of experienced market practitioners and run a series of tests using an ethical-evaluation matrix.

The regulator's view

Regulation covering market abuse is to be found in most major markets. US and UK securities regulation clearly prohibits price manipulation and trading based on inside information, but there is a regulatory grey area around the issue of predatory trading that is designed to move prices and thus precipitate an automatic response from other traders; and around the sources of the information used to motivate predatory trades.

> " Empirical evidence shows that predators impose economically significant losses on index funds. "

Predatory trading would be legally prohibited where it involved the use of inside information or where it was deemed to constitute market abuse, but would otherwise be legal. This suggests that some forms of predatory trading might be legal; and others not.

In the UK, the FSA Code of Market Conduct prohibits some forms of front-running/pre-positioning, but permits others. It defines front-running as

> ... a transaction for a person's own benefit on the basis of and ahead of an order which he is to carry out with or for another (in respect of which information concerning the order is inside information), which takes advantage of the anticipated impact of the order on the market price. (FSA MAR 1: 1.3.2 Descriptions of behaviour that amount to market abuse (insider dealing).)

Trading ahead of others based on signals observable in the trading pit is legal. The distinguishing factor between these two cases is the existence or otherwise of inside information.

Cai (2003) identifies a regulatory grey area:

Any market maker who knows that a specific order is "overhanging the market" can exploit this information to make a speculative profit in the short run. Such advance knowledge of the future order flow can turn the market maker into a 'virtual' insider, even without information about the fundamental value of the security.

The industry body for investment analysts and managers, the CFA Institute, introduced in the ninth edition (2005) of its *Standards of Practice Handbook* a section on market manipulation (Standard II, Integrity of Capital Markets (B), Market Manipulation). It argues that

market manipulation damages the interests of all investors by disrupting the smooth functioning of financial markets and damaging investor confidence.

The code describes information-based manipulation (i.e. the release of false information for the implementation of pump-and-dump strategies) and transaction-based manipulation (e.g. transactions that artificially distort prices or volume to give the impression of activity or price movement in a financial instrument; and securing a controlling or dominant position in a financial instrument to exploit and manipulate the price of a related derivative and/or the underlying asset). The handbook makes no specific mention of predatory behaviour.

The standard does not prohibit "legitimate trading strategies that exploit a difference in market power, information, or other market inefficiencies" and states that "the intent of the action is critical to determining whether it is a violation of this standard."

It would be extremely difficult for a third-party observer, such as a regulator, to differentiate between a bona fide informed investment-decision and a manipulative trade, solely by examining short-run trading data. Both should result in high trading volume followed by abnormally high (or low) stock returns. In practice, regulators and lawyers attempt to identify the motivation for specific transactions by making use of software tools that search for meaning in email trails and other unstructured data.

In general, regulation does not prohibit trading aimed at exploiting the predictable trade patterns of others. Nor does it prohibit trading aimed at exploiting public information about a trader's proximity to financial distress. Nevertheless, some ambiguity remains. Commenting on a 2005 case in which the UK financial regulator fined an investment bank following an investigation into transaction-based manipulation, UK law firm Freshfields Bruckhaus Deringer argued that

> the FSA decision raised serious issues for all firms whose business involves executing large trades which have the potential significantly to move the market price or reduce liquidity.

As shown earlier, predatory trading is *designed* to reduce liquidity. As such, regulatory-enforcement history casts at least some doubt as to its legality.

What about the ethics of predatory trading?

Does *ethical* behaviour simply amount to following securities law? Not according to Szego (2006), who argues that

> there is no strict relationship between ethics and law. Unethical acts could be legal and vice-versa.

This view was echoed by one of my interviewees:

> I don't think that the law defines the limits of ethics...I think that ethics generally move in ways that cannot be easily captured by regulatory frameworks, so I would say that it is probably not

practical to expect regulation to take into account all the ethical issues and boundaries.

But should traders even be concerned with ethics?

Lorenzo (2006) argues that cost-benefit evaluation, rather than ethical compliance, is the main determinant of corporate behaviour. However, McCosh (1999) argues that "ethics is one of the lifelines that protects

> " It would be extremely difficult for a third party observer, such as a regulator, to differentiate between a bona fide informed investment-decision and a manipulative trade, solely by examining short-run trading data. "

capital market workers from the temptation to cut corners". He believes that unethical conduct is unsustainable in the long run and that ethicality is paramount for a successful career in finance.

Dobson (2005) argues that,

> as a financial analyst or other finance professional, you act entirely
> naturally and in your self-interest by nurturing a genuine concern
> for the client, the professional body, professional associates, and
> so on. It is natural for you to have these group-oriented concerns,
> and the ethics code can nurture these natural tendencies.

Interviewees expressed a range of views on the ethics of predatory trading. At one extreme were those who claimed to practise predatory trading and spoke openly about their tactics; others did not practise it but argued that investors are "consenting adults" and that markets need show no mercy to the naïve. A number stated that they were aware of predatory trading but did not wish to jeopardise their firms' reputation by practicing it.

Different ethical perspectives

Next, I examine predatory trading from a series of ethical perspectives. Each of these provides a framework for thinking about the ethics of an action.

Virtue ethics

The first of these is 'virtue ethics', which evolved in ancient Greece and is mainly associated with Aristotle. It comprises a set of characteristics to be developed and followed by an individual, so as to guarantee the adequate resolution of ethical problems. In includes the Platonic virtues of wisdom, courage, self-control and justice, plus qualities such as truthfulness, magnanimity, patience and liberality. Aristotle considered 'justice' to be the greatest of virtues. Moral virtue comes about as a result of 'habit', as distinct from 'nature'. Virtue ethics are also reflected in a series of religious moral codes.

MacIntyre (1987) has been one of the main proponents of the central role of virtues in moral philosophy. He is skeptical about modern finance managers' abilities to practise virtuous behaviour. Predatory trading would fail on the most important of the virtues – justice – as the prey is deliberately exploited by the predator.

An aspect of predatory trading that separates it from other forms of trading is that its market impact can precipitate action in others, by moving prices (sometimes only slightly) towards the trigger point for a forced or anticipated trade by the prey. Thus, predatory trading in a sense coerces others into trading, an aspect that would raise strong objections from a philosopher such as Kant. He established the concept of the categorical imperative, an unconditional command of reason that must be obeyed without exception. It includes the notion that one should treat the humanity in a person as an end, and never merely as a means.

Bowie (1998) argues that if the principle on which a business action is based passes the test of the categorical imperative, it can be viewed as a moral action. He identifies two types of Kantian freedom: negative (i.e. freedom from coercion and deception) and positive (i.e. freedom to develop one's human capacities). Application of these requires that people in a business relationship be neither coerced nor deceived, and that business practices contribute to the development of rational and moral capacities. Predatory trading that precipitates action in others would breach Kant's 'freedom from coercion' principle. Where the prey is a *known* individual, predatory trading also fails to treat the humanity in the person as an end.

Consequentialist perspective

A consequentialist perspective on ethics focuses on the consequences or results of a decision or action. An example is Utilitarianism[13] according to which an ethical act should maximise benefits to society and minimise harms.

This is a calculating approach to ethics, where calculations can be expressed in purely economic or monetary terms. A utilitarian might initially consider predatory trading to be morally neutral as the prey's loss is balanced by the predator's gain. However, predatory trading has the potential for price destabilisation, with negative consequences for pricing efficiency and confidence amongst market participants.

Luetge (2005) argues that traditional ethics are ill-suited to handling modern business problems. He proposes that mutual benefits be considered in any assessment, which is at the core of the "social contract theory" of Hobbs, Spinoza and Rawls. This requires the calculation of advantages by taking a long-run rather than a short-term perspective,

---

[13] See Bentham (1843).

and taking a social rather than an individual view. Predatory trading would likely fail these criteria in light of its potentially destabilizing influence and liquidity effects, and the impact this has on confidence in the market as a whole.

Contractualism

Toenjis (2002) argues that contractualism is the most realistic ethical approach to business. He envisages co-operation which is free, equal, reasonable, and rational. Quite possibly, professional investors could jointly agree on the acceptability of predatory trading, on condition that there was no abuse of insider information. One interviewee commented:

> It's important that there are rules of engagement in any market, and that those rules of engagement are stuck to by the participants of those markets. Principles-based [terms of engagement] is better than rules-based. So long as we have a set of principles and everyone follows them, then that should be absolutely fine.

However, consider the case of retail investors in, say, an open-ended fund that has performed poorly and was suffering from redemptions. Where predators were exploiting this situation, it is highly unlikely that fund investors would ever find such behaviour acceptable.

In summary, predatory trading appears to be unethical when viewed from each of the perspectives above.

But should we expect market participants to behave ethically in the sense meant by ethicists?

Velasquez (1997) argues that

> while some moral norms are so immediately related to the fundamental good that they are universally binding, other moral norms are derivative and subject to cultural and historical variability.

A theory developed by Donaldson and Dunfee (1994) known as 'Integrated Social Contracts Theory' (ISCT) emphasises the role of communities in generating moral norms. The convergence of religious, cultural and philosophical beliefs around certain core principles helps to identify a series of 'hypernorms' that provide a moral foundation for business. ISCT also recognises the existence of culturally distinct microsocial contracts that operate within this foundation.

Schneider (2000) criticizes the application of ethical monism in applied ethics, arguing that ethical principles may conflict and that not all monist theories may be applicable to specific decision-making situations. Furthermore, a richness of ethical theories can assist in forming moral judgments in novel situations. He thus proposes a moral pluralist approach. Taking account of this, and the ideas incorporated within ISCT, I form a framework below for testing the ethics of predatory trading practices.

A framework for testing the ethics of predatory trading practices

I analyse examples of predatory trading and their context (i.e. the actors and circumstances) by making use of an ethical-evaluation matrix, similar to that produced by Fisher and Lovell (2006). This approach involves the consideration of a specific situation from the perspective of several ethical theories at a time. It allows for judgment to be made about the importance of each ethical theory with respect to the behaviour being evaluated. I use findings from my interviews with practitioners to assist in completing the evaluation matrix.

In the matrix, each criterion is ascribed one of four levels of importance.

1. **Trigger** level – a criterion is so important that a decision can be taken on the basis of this criterion alone.

2. **Veto** level – a veto decision can be taken *against action* on the basis of this criterion, but it is not strong enough to trigger a positive action.

3. **Ordinary** level – a criterion should be considered, but is not so critical as to be a 'trigger' or 'veto' level decision.

4. **Reject** level – a criterion is not applicable or important to the decision being taken.

A series of ethical theories are considered in the matrix, and an assessment is made as to whether the action would be perceived positively or negatively under each theory in turn. These ethical tests include:

•   **Light-of-day Test**. How would I feel if my decision and actions became public knowledge?

•   **Virtuous Mean Test**. Does the decision add to, or detract from, the creation of a virtuous life?

•   **Veil of Ignorance/Golden Rule**. If I were to take the place of one of those affected by my decision or action, how would I then regard the act?

- **Universality Test.** If my decision or action became a universal principle applicable to all in similar situations, would the results be positive or negative?

- **Communitarian Test.** Would my actions help or hinder the community to develop ethically?

- **Self-interest Test.** Does the decision meet my own interests and values?

- **Consequential Test.** As a whole, are the anticipated consequences of my decision positive or negative?

- **Discourse Test.** Has the issue been properly discussed and have the appropriate people been involved?

After taking account of trigger and veto criteria, the sum of positives and negatives from the ordinary level is calculated to identify the appropriate ethical position. It is, of course, possible to undertake variations of this analysis, or to make the analysis more complex, such as prioritising the ethical principles.

Example

As an illustration, consider the case of an integrated investment bank's proprietary trading desk that has obtained publicly available information about financial distress in a fund that uses the bank's brokerage services. The investment bank considers the ethics of undertaking predatory trading against the fund.

The bank would not wish it to be known that it had traded against one of its own customers, and so the light-of-day test is negative. The virtuous mean test is made a reject-level decision, on the basis that it is not the role of securities markets to provide a model of virtue. The proprietary trading desk would not wish to find itself in the position of the prey, and so the Golden Rule is scored negatively. The universality test is scored positively, as it is possible for predatory trading to become a universal principle in securities markets. Predatory trading does not help the ethical development of the market community or individuals, and so fails the communitarian test. The self-interest test could score in either direction, but on the assumption that the present value of the immediate trading profit exceeds the present value of all future benefits accruing from the client relationship in question, it is scored positively. The consequentialist test is scored negatively, as abnormal profits and losses balance in the market, but the market could be temporarily destabilised during the predation process. The discourse test is scored negatively, as all relevant parties have not debated this issue in a full and appropriate manner. The results are summarised below in Table 2.3.

Table 2.3: Ethical test matrix for example case

	Reject	Veto	Trigger	Positive	Negative
Virtue Ethics					
1. Light-of-Day test					-
2. Virtuous mean test	Y				
Deontological ethics					
3. Veil of ignorance test/ Golden Rule					-
4. Universality test				+	
Ethical Learning and Growth					
5. Communitarian test					-
6. Self-interest test				+	
Consequentialist ethics					
7. Consequential test					-
8. Discourse test					-

From the matrix, we have two positive and five negative outcomes, resulting in a negative ethical decision for the practice being considered.

Changing the player

If I replace the integrated investment bank with a hedge fund and re-run the tests, I find that the light-of-day test and also the discourse test now become positive. Whereas an integrated investment bank, serving the needs of its different client types as well as trading with its own capital, might be reticent in revealing the true nature of its proprietary trading activities, a hedge fund might feel comfortable revealing its true nature – it is designed, amongst other things, to exploit weaknesses in other actors' behaviour. The matrix would show four positive and three negative outcomes, resulting in a positive decision.

Changing the nature of the information

We can also change the nature of the information obtained by the hedge fund. If the information about financial distress was a market rumour of financial distress, rather than public information, then the light-of-day, and discourse tests become more marginal decisions. The source of the information (whether it was inferred from market behaviour or obtained via a breach of confidence) would be a relevant factor in this example. Where information being used is inside information, the action becomes illegal; the light-of-day, discourse and also universality tests would score negatively and the final decision becomes negative.

This matrix can be used to evaluate some of the more morally ambivalent aspects of predatory trading. For example, we know from the Brunnermeier and Pedersen model that collusion, either explicit or tacit, amongst predators can enhance its profitability. But is such collusion ethical? We also know (from the Attari *et al.* model) that lending to prey when the latter is financially distressed can be used to prolong the opportunity for predatory trading against them – rather like a cat toying with a mouse, just before the kill.

From the ethical-evaluation matrix, I find that the ethics of a predatory trading strategy depends on the relationship between the actors involved and the nature in which information is obtained about the prey.

Furthermore, the dominant view that emerged from interviews was that predatory trading should not harm one's own clients and that information should be fairly acquired (i.e. not acquired through a breach of a firewall).

Chinese walls

Integrated investment banks make use of firewalls (or 'Chinese walls') to prevent information about clients flowing from one division to another. However, there was considerable skepticism amongst interviewees about the effectiveness of these, and about the source of information used to drive predatory trading strategies. Zaloom (2006), in her description of trading on Chicago's CBOT, describes how

> occasionally a broker may illegally expose his deck [of trades], doling out coveted information to a favored trader. Social loyalties and exchange of favors exist alongside brokers' responsibilities to act as the agents of outside buyers and sellers.

In addition, social interactions amongst arbitrageurs and investment bankers are an everyday part of the functioning of markets. Information on client trading patterns or their capital resources is unlikely to remain fully confidential under such circumstances, and a number of interviewees argued, using first-hand examples, that firewalls did not always work properly.

> " The ethics of a predatory trading strategy depend on the relationship between the actors involved and the nature in which information is obtained about the prey. "

At what point does information about a client's impending financial distress evolve from confidential client information through to market rumour and then on to generally accepted knowledge? One interviewee argued:

> since the market began there have been rumours, even under the Buttonwood tree no doubt. People are going to deal on that basis. How do you distinguish a rumour from a feeling from an insight? You can't do it. You couldn't rule that out.

By bringing together legal, regulatory and industry pronouncements, feedback from experienced market practitioners and the results of tests using the Fisher and Lovell ethical-evaluation matrix, it is possible to arrive at a 'verdict' or 'view' on the ethics of predatory trading.

- **Predatory trading is ethical** when it is based on publicly available or inferable information; the predators are truthful in their dealings with others; and the predator firm's clients are not harmed.

- **Predatory trading is unethical** if it harms the firm's own clients; if the predator is untruthful about his activities; or if the information driving the strategy is obtained through a breach of a firewall.

CHAPTER 3

CROWDED EXITS

Consider the following situation. You are a short-seller and have identified a highly leveraged firm that is exposed to the general health of the economy. The firm has pared down costs in the past few years (and so has limited potential for further efficiencies). Management is well regarded and the high stock price reflects their achievements to date. But now the economy is starting to slow...

The stock price begins to fall from its peak and you anticipate that this could be the start of a trend. You short the stock. The stock continues to fall and your short position moves into profit. You sell more. Other short-sellers begin to notice the same opportunity and short-interest rises.

The stock price is now falling precipitately as the economy enters recession. The market capitalisation of the firm's equity has become very small compared to its debt. More short-sellers have joined the feeding frenzy, so that 16% of the firm's stock is out on loan. In fact, it is now difficult to work out what the equity is worth, as much depends on whether or not the firm survives in its current form. Will there be asset sales, a large rights issue, or even a debt-for-equity swap? Or could the firm muddle through if the economy were to recover soon?

Next, some macro-economic data is published suggesting that the rate of decline in the economy is slowing. The market realises that recoveries start with this type of data release, and the general desire to avoid risk amongst equity investors is replaced by a desire to buy shares in distressed companies with recovery potential. The stock price of the company rises by 20% in a couple of days. Your short position is still comfortably in profit, but for those who started to short the stock only recently (and there are many of these!) the loss is very painful.

Some of these short-sellers place buy orders in the market, in an attempt to cover their positions. This new source of demand causes the stock price to rise by another 20%. Now other recent short-sellers are beginning to suffer losses. Will they cover too? But looking at the number of shares on loan (and thus potentially sold short) relative to normal trading volume, it becomes clear to you that not all short-sellers can cover their positions at the same time at the prevailing stock price. The image in your mind is of an audience in a crowded theatre rushing to a narrow exit door as the fire alarm sounds…only so many can leave the building in any given interval of time.

So, should you join the rush to the door and try to get out now, or wait and suffer losses?

And what exactly is each share in the company worth right now? Meanwhile, the stock price is still rising…

Punch Taverns

Below are two charts for Punch Taverns, a UK leisure company that attracted much short interest in 2008 and early 2009.

Notice from Figure 3.1 how, as the stock price fell, the percentage of shares outstanding on loan grew strongly through mid-2008. If all borrowed shares had been sold short, then those short positions would have been equivalent, at the peak, to about 50 days of normal trading volume in the stock (see Figure 3.2). This looks very much like a 'crowded short' position.

You can also see from Figure 3.1 that the share price rose sharply from a low base in April 2009 (in fact, it quadrupled from its low point in less than a month). The number of shares on loan fell meaningfully around the same time. There was thus large-scale short covering into a rapidly rising share price – this would have been a painful episode for some short-sellers.

Figure 3.1 - Percentage of shares outstanding on loan for Punch Taverns (April 2007 – April 2009)

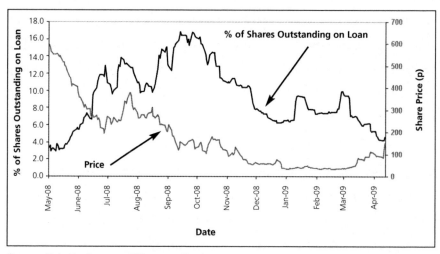

Source: Data Explorers and Thomson Reuters

Figure 3.2 - Ratio of the number of shares on loan to the normal number of shares traded each day (days to cover ratio) for Punch Taverns (April 2007 – 2009)

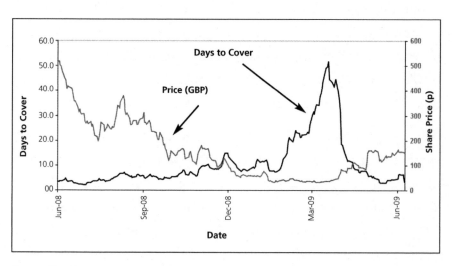

Source: Data Explorers and Thomson Reuters

Crowded exits like this are a liquidity problem faced by short-sellers. Crowded exits arise in stocks where short-sellers hold large positions relative to normal trading volume, and when a catalyst prompts short-sellers to cover their positions rapidly and simultaneously. The temporary excess of demand for stock relative to normal trading volume leads to upward pressure on the stock price. As a result, these events are associated with losses to short-sellers.

As part of any description of crowded exits, it is helpful to explain how a short position might become 'crowded' in the first instance. Just now, I described how a firm with leveraged exposure to a weakening economy, combined with a falling share price, attracted large numbers of short-sellers. A different scenario is outlined below.

Rational imitation strategy

Consider initially that one or more traders with negative information about a company short-sell stock in that company. This represents informed trading and leads to an increase in the number of shares shorted. This increase in short-interest is made public, as most developed stock markets require the publication of data on short-selling or stock lending, in the interests of transparency.

Now, a substantial body of empirical research shows that heavily shorted stocks perform poorly[14]. Market participants who are aware of this evidence can simply short-sell stocks that are seen to be heavily shorted, in an attempt to benefit from the short-sellers' information. Where this type of rational imitation strategy occurs in markets, it follows that heavily shorted stock positions contain both informed traders and noise traders. However, strategies like this contain the seeds of their own destruction. In this illustration, imitation leads to an

---

[14] See, for example, Diether *et al.*, 2009 and Boehmer *et al.*, 2008.

increase in the size of the short position relative to the liquidity of the stock. A crowded short position thus develops, based on a mix of informed short-selling and rational imitation.

I refer to short positions that are large relative to normal trading volume as 'crowded positions'. With a catalyst, rapid and simultaneous short-covering can commence and the crowded position becomes a 'crowded exit'.

Causes of crowded exits

A variety of catalysts for a crowded exit are possible:

- a company could release new, positive information to the market,

- a sell-side analyst could upgrade his earnings forecast or trading recommendation on a stock,

- informed short-sellers could receive new, private information and start to cover their positions, to be followed by imitators.

Another catalyst could be that short-sellers become unable to hold on to their short positions and so must cover these positions. This could be due to stock loan recall, client redemptions, margin calls or risk control mechanisms. This short covering could be misconstrued as informed buying and so act as a catalyst for short covering by imitators.

Finally, manipulators buying shares in a company could prompt short covering amongst traders who misinterpret the manipulative trades as informed buying.

From interviews with practitioners, I find that short-sellers perceive crowded exits to be an important risk: it could become difficult to cover a short position when desired, or the short-seller could suffer losses due to market impact for demanding liquidity to cover a short position quickly.

To explore crowded exits and other liquidity problems in more detail, I have built a dataset based on UK equities and used it to investigate patterns in stock returns and stock-lending activity that are consistent with crowded exits. The results should improve our understanding of these events and provide evidence that could help traders to manage liquidity risk.

Data

To examine this topic more closely, I merge data from two sources to create a new dataset. The first of these sources is a commercial database of UK stock-lending data from Index Explorers Ltd. This contains daily stock lending information (including shares on loan) starting on 3 September 2003 when the database came into existence. At inception, this database included stocks from the 350 largest companies traded on the London Stock Exchange. The data is sourced from CREST – the organisation responsible for settlement of all trades on the London Stock Exchange. The amount of stock on loan is updated daily, but with a three-day reporting lag[15]. Over time, the coverage of companies in the database increased through the addition of smaller capitalisation stocks so that by the end date for this sample, 31 May 2007, there is stock-lending data for 681 companies.

The smallest of these companies have market capitalizations of approximately £25 million as of 2007. A number of companies cease to exist at some point during the 45 months (979 trading days) studied. This could be as a result of a merger or acquisition, the lapsing of the company into administrative receivership, or a change to private ownership. These companies are included in the database until the date of their de-listing, to prevent survivor bias.

---

[15] Before 12 December 2005, the reporting lag was five days.

The second source is Datastream, which provides daily stock returns, free-float percentage of shares[16] and fundamental data on each stock.

I merge the two databases, and construct a new dataset that includes stock return, trading, lending and fundamental information for up to 681 stocks listed on the London Stock Exchange, for the 979 trading days between 3 September 2003 and 31 May 2007.

Using stock-lending data to examine the risks in short-selling

Direct data on short-selling is not publicly available in the UK. Instead, daily stock-lending data is available. Stock-lending acts as a proxy for short-selling, as the process of short-selling generally requires stock to be borrowed to facilitate settlement of the trade.

However, there are a number of problems with using stock lending data as a proxy for short-selling. First, shares do not need to be borrowed to undertake naked short-selling. Secondly, stock-lending occurs for a number of reasons other than short-selling, including dividend tax arbitrage, financing purposes and vote-buying.

One of the crucial issues for this study concerns the time around the dividend dates. Dividend-paying stocks often experience large increases in shares on loan around divided record dates, indicating a dividend capture effect that is consistent with dividend tax arbitrage. To minimise the risk that stock-lending for dividend tax arbitrage is confounded with borrowing to facilitate short-selling, I remove data from three weeks before until three weeks after the dividend record date for each stock in this study of stock-lending data.

---

[16] Free-float percentage of shares is defined as the percentage of the total number of shares in issue that are available to ordinary investors, i.e. that are not held away from the market by government or close family interests.

A third limitation on the use of stock lending data as a proxy for short-selling is the extent to which market practitioners fail to fulfil their obligations to report stock-lending to the market authorities. Discussions with practitioners involved in stock lending suggest that this problem is rare, but unavoidable.

Finally, derivatives can be used to effect transactions that are economically equivalent to short-selling. The extent to which the use of derivatives to facilitate short-selling is transmitted into the stock-lending market influences the usefulness of stock-lending data as a proxy for short-selling. Discussions with stock-lending practitioners suggests that the majority, but not all, short-sale-equivalent trades using derivatives are ultimately hedged by the counter parties to those trades, through borrowing stock and selling short.

The dataset used for this study incorporates daily data on shares borrowed and stock returns, and so offers an appropriate degree of granularity for examining short-selling risks such as crowded exits.

Crowded positions

To identify a crowded exit, I need first a method for identifying a 'crowded position' and second, a formal definition for 'rapid and simultaneous' short covering. Where these occur together, this constitutes a crowded exit.

Days-to-cover ratio

I start by measuring the ratio of shares on loan to the normal trading volume for each stock on each day (i.e. for each firm day). This is called the 'days-to-cover ratio' (or DCR). The DCR is a liquidity ratio: the higher this ratio, the more difficult it should be for short-sellers to liquidate their positions without having market impact. The ratio is calculated as:

$$\text{Days to Cover Ratio}_{i,t} \ (DCR) = \frac{\text{Shares on Loan}_{i,t}}{\text{Average Daily Trading Volume}_{i,t}} \quad (3.1)$$

$\text{Shares on Loan}_{i,t}$ is the closing number of shares on loan for stock i on day t.

$\text{Average Daily Trading Volume}_{i,t}$ is the moving average of the number of shares traded for stock i from days (t-61) to (t-1).[17]

For each day, I rank stocks by their DCR and construct three portfolios containing the 99th, 95th, and 90th percentile, of stocks by DCR. These higher percentiles represent the most 'crowded' short positions. A prerequisite of a crowded exit is that the stock should have a high level of short interest relative to its liquidity, and this simple sort captures that condition.

---

[17] I choose 60 days of trading volume as a compromise between the risk of including outdated information on trading volume and the risk of one or more exceptional days influencing the moving-average figure.

The portfolio characteristics resulting from these simple sorts are shown in Table 3.1.

Table 3.1 - Portfolios based on simple sorts

This table reports the characteristics of portfolios sorted daily by days-to-cover Ratio (DCR) over the period 1 September 2003 to 31 May 2007. DCR is calculated as shares on loan divided by average daily trading volume. The first column shows variables for the entire sample, the following three columns show the 99th, 95th, and 90th percentiles by DCR respectively. Past return is calculated as the raw percentage return of each portfolio over the previous 20 trading days.

		All	99th Percentile DCR>19.4	95th Percentile DCR>12.4	90th Percentile DCR>8.11
Panel A. Short Interest					
DCR (days)	Mean	7.88	147.26	52.87	34.71
	Median	4.48	62.68	25.76	19.36
	Std. Dev	29.29	224.63	119.21	86.97
Shares on Loan (in millions)	Mean	23.39	25.90	26.31	33.17
	Median	4.40	14.10	7.80	9.40
	Std. Dev	74.99	63.48	58.36	67.72
Mkt Cap on Loan (%)	Mean	2.90	5.60	6.22	6.20
	Median	1.84	3.54	4.66	4.90
	Std. Dev	3.07	4.19	4.39	4.52
Free Float on Loan (%)	Mean	4.68	9.82	10.77	10.66
	Median	2.70	6.75	7.76	7.93
	Std. Dev	5.68	7.93	9.05	9.04
Panel B. Stock Liquidity					
Turnover by shares (in millions)	Mean	3.24	0.45	1.21	1.94
	Median	0.31	0.10	0.16	0.26
	Std. Dev	15.74	2.10	3.82	5.35
Free Float (%)	Mean	66.54	65.34	66.07	66.64
	Median	69.00	65.00	68.00	69.00
	Std. Dev	21.64	21.64	20.00	20.42
Panel C. Other Stock Charactersistics					
Volatility	Mean	0.24	0.25	0.24	0.25
	Median	0.22	0.22	0.22	0.23
	Std. Dev	0.14	0.14	0.12	0.12
Mkt Cap (in millions)	Mean	2294	697	983	1574
	Median	370	444	443	499
	Std. Dev	8485	3740	2980	5093
Book to Market ratio	Mean	0.67	6.21	1.86	1.21
	Median	0.48	0.47	0.55	0.49
	Std. Dev	037.91	15.36	7.68	5.52
Past Return (%)	Mean	1.93	2.23	1.41	1.49
	Median	1.60	1.67	1.34	1.36
	Std. Dev	8.37	8.72	7.81	7.60

Unsurprisingly, the higher DCR percentiles have higher short-interest than the average stock – around twice as much. Furthermore, turnover by shares is generally poorer in portfolios with higher DCRs. Thus, a high DCR typically results from the combination of high short interest and poorer liquidity. We can also see that crowded positions tend to occur in smaller stocks.

There is no apparent relationship between volatility and DCR. The higher DCR portfolios exhibit greater median, but lower mean, market capitalizations in comparison to the whole sample. The higher DCR portfolios exhibit median book-to-market ratios that are similar to that of the whole sample, although the mean book-to-market ratios are greater, suggesting skew in the distribution of this ratio. There is also no apparent relationship between past returns and DCR

Returns on the high DCR portfolios

Next, I calculate the returns associated with these portfolios of high DCR stocks. This allows me to investigate the aggregate losses to short-sellers who cannot or do not cover their positions. Portfolio returns could be influenced by the riskiness of the stocks in the portfolio. To accommodate this possibility, I adjust stock returns for risk by using the capital asset pricing model to estimate *abnormal returns*[18]. I calculate equal-weighted cumulative abnormal returns (CAR) for each portfolio resulting from a sort over a series of holding periods.

In measuring these abnormal returns, I skip one day and hold the portfolios over N=1, 5, 10, 20 and 60 trading days. Skipping a day

---

[18] Results in this empirical research space have been uniformly robust to changes in asset-pricing model and so in this research, I choose to use the CAPM model for its simplicity. To facilitate the estimation of abnormal stock returns using an asset-pricing model, I collect daily stock returns for the year before the start of the Index Explorers database. This 'formation period' runs from 1 September 2002 to, 1 September 2003 and the daily stock returns collected are used to estimate the beta of each stock in the study.

reduces the risk that stock prices are disproportionately at either bid or ask – this problem can plague some empirical studies (and is known as the 'bid-ask bounce problem').

As cumulative abnormal returns for periods of up to 60 days are estimated for each day, there is thus a problem of overlapping data to address. This can lead to biased results.[19] To solve this problem whilst making full use of the daily data, I use a calendar-time portfolio approach to calculate average daily returns[20].

Table 3.2 - Presents the cumulative abnormal returns associated with portfolios of stocks where short positions are 'crowded'

The table reports cumulative abnormal returns (CAR) for higher-percentile DCR portfolios from 1 Sep 2003 to 31 May 2007. Stocks are sorted into 99th, 95th, and 90th percentiles based on their days-to-cover Ratio. Portfolios are re-balanced daily. By skipping one day to avoid concerns about bid-ask bounce, cumulative abnormal returns and t-statistics are calculated using a calendar-time approach with a holding period of 1, 5, 10, 20 and 60 trading days. All returns are quoted as percentages.

		99th Percentile	95th percentile	90th Percentile
AR(+1)	Mean	0.034	0.020	0.027
	t-Stat	1.345	1.720 *	2.429
CAR(+5)	Mean	0.127	0.127	0.116
	t-Stat	1.188	2.710***	2.951***
CAR(+10)	Mean	0.291	0.307	0.263
	t-Stat	1.032	3.250***	3.423***
CAR(+20)	Mean	0.348	0.562	0.622
	t-Stat	1.742*	2.989***	4.265***
CAR(+60)	Mean	2.027	1.203	1.463
	t-Stat	1.682*	1.970**	3.419**

Note: *indicates significance at 10% level, **indicates significance at 5% level, and ***indicates significance at 1% level.

---

[19] Estimates based on overlapping periods could capture autocorrelation and heteroskedasticity in a firm's excess returns, thus biasing the results. Since I rank by DCR daily and hold portfolios for N subsequent days, I need to adjust for unknown autocorrelation and heteroskedasticity in returns.

[20] A calendar-time portfolio approach is a two-step procedure. The first step involves calculating an average return for a cross-section of stocks and the second step measures the risk-adjusted performance by estimating a time-series regression model.

These results reveal positive abnormal returns for each of the higher DCR portfolios over the majority of the time periods considered. Statistical significance is generally stronger over the longer holding periods; and for the 90th and 95th percentiles compared to the 99th percentile. This latter effect is due to the lower volatility of abnormal returns in the 90th and 95th percentile portfolios, such that statistical significance can be established at a lower abnormal return.

Crowded exits

Not all crowded positions represent crowded exits. For example, where a position is crowded, short-sellers might simply unwind their positions gradually and with little market impact. They might even add to their short positions in the near term. We are interested in the subset of crowded positions where there is also rapid and simultaneous (i.e. exceptional) short covering.

Methodology for identifying exceptional short covering

To identify these, I use simultaneous sorts: I sort stocks into 99th, 95th, and 90th percentiles based on DCR, and narrow down the portfolios by controlling for exceptional changes in short interest on the previous day. The resulting portfolios contain stocks experiencing crowded exits.

To define an 'exceptional' reduction in short interest level, note that only publicly-traded stocks are generally loaned and so it is important to consider each firm's free float, rather than total shares outstanding. I first calculate the change in the free float on loan for each stock on each day. I then calculate the average change across all stocks for any given day.

I divide the daily change in free float on loan for stock i ($CFFL_{i,t}$) by the market average change ($CFFLm,t$) to obtain the daily change in free float on loan relative to the market average change, as shown in the equation below:

Relative daily change for stock i $(RCFFL_{i,t}) = \dfrac{CFFL_{i,t}}{CFFL_{m,t}}$ (3.2)

Next, I test whether or not each is 'exceptional'.

For each firm day, I calculate $RCFFL_{i,t}$ for the 20 previous days and measure the mean and standard deviation of this series. I identify situations where $RCFFL_{i,t}$ is greater than 2 standard deviations away from its mean. Where this occurs at the same time as a fall in shares on loan, I regard this as an exceptional decrease in the level of short interest.

I separate each of the crowded position portfolios into two sub-sets:

1. a 'crowded-exit portfolio' (where each stock experiences an exceptional decrease in short interest) and

2. a 'not crowded-exit portfolio'.

I find that, on average, a crowded-exit portfolio comprises stocks exhibiting dramatically lower mean (and median) trading volumes. This suggests that liquidity is important in explaining crowded-exits. The book-to-market ratio is also much lower for a crowded exit portfolio, suggesting that these comprise glamour (as opposed to value) stocks[21].

RNS announcements

I examine each of the stocks appearing in a crowded exit portfolio to identify if there are regulatory news service releases around the time of the crowded exit. In approximately half the cases, there are regulatory news announcements in the period from seven days before the start of exceptional short covering. This suggests that public, company-specific

---

[21] Glamour stocks can be characterised as those with high ratios of market capitalisation to book value; value stocks as those with low ratios.

news could be the catalyst for some, but not all, crowded exits. Stocks typically stay in a crowded-exit portfolio for a limited number of days (a mean of 3.35 days for the 99th percentile portfolios, 3.55 days for the 95th percentile portfolios and 4.45 days for the 90th percentile portfolios).

Filtering possible arbitrage stocks

Not all short sales are motivated by negative opinions on a stock. For example, short-sellers might short stocks to conduct convertibles arbitrage and so take advantage of relative mis-pricing between a stock and a convertible bond issued by the same company. Where a short-seller is arbitrage-motivated, he will be partially hedged against adverse movements in the stock price and so less likely to cover his position in response to a crowded exit. The presence of such arbitrageurs could thus obfuscate our results and weaken the power of any tests. I use Thomson One Banker to identify firms with convertible bonds as part of their capital structure. I separate those firms with convertible bonds from those without. Approximately one fifth of stocks in the panel have convertibles within their capital structure.

Estimating cumulative abnormal returns

Having indentified portfolios of stocks experiencing crowded exits, and having separated stocks with convertible bonds in their capital structure from those without, I now estimate cumulative abnormal returns for the resulting portfolios. I employ the same procedure to estimate CARs as described earlier.

I expect greater CARs for the non-convertible portfolios compared to the convertible portfolios, as short positions in the non-convertible portfolios are not hedged by long positions in convertible bonds. And indeed, I find greater CARs for the non-convertible portfolios in every case. For the portfolios of stocks that contain convertible bonds within their capital structure, almost all the CARs are statistically insignificant.

Results for crowded exit portfolios for firms *without* convertibles in their capital structure are shown in Table 3.3.

Table 3.3 - Abnormal Returns around Crowded Exits

The table reports cumulative abnormal returns (CAR) for crowded-exit portfolios from 1 September 2003 to 31 May 2007. Any company with a convertible bond in its capital structure is identified as being exposed to arbitrage-motivated short-selling and eliminated from the sample, leaving only portfolios of companies without convertible bonds in their capital structure. By skipping one day to avoid concerns about bid-ask bounce, cumulative abnormal returns and t-statistics are calculated using a calendar-time approach with a holding period of 1, 5, 10, 20 and 60 trading days. All returns are quoted as percentages.

		99th Percentile	*95th percentile*	*90th Percentile*
AR(+1)	Mean	0.728	0.190	0.167
	t-Stat	1.117	1.295	1.895*
CAR(+5)	Mean	2.350	0.494	0.466
	t-Stat	0.096	0.825	1.443
CAR(+10)	Mean	6.106	1.327	1.095
	t-Stat	2.279**	1.815*	2.120*
CAR(+20)	Mean	8.083	3.763	3.589
	t-Stat	2.235**	2.571**	3.974***
CAR(+60)	Mean	26.981	8.312	5.514
	t-Stat	2.508**	1.949*	1.967*

Note: *indicates significance at 10% level, **indicates significance at 5% level, and ***indicates significance at 1% level.

Results

All of the crowded-exit portfolios have positive CARs, most of which are statistically significant. We might expect the abnormal returns from crowded-exit portfolios to be greater than those from simple crowded position portfolios and a comparison between the two tables bears this out.

For example, the highest CAR for a crowded-exit portfolio is observed in the 99th percentile over the holding period of 60 trading days; at almost 27% it is statistically significant at the 5% level. By contrast, the equivalent 'crowded position' portfolio exhibits a CAR only slightly greater than 2% and only significant at the 10% level.

Although the positive CARs are not statistically significant over shorter periods, they are all statistically significant over periods of ten days or greater. The mean CAR for the 99th percentile crowded-exit portfolios held over 60 days is also economically significant. This indicates potentially large losses for short-sellers during crowded exits. Stocks in the 99th percentile-portfolio have an average DCR of over 147 days, and so it is unsurprising that such stocks could remain crowded even after 60 days.

These results are consistent with the notion that crowded exits are a risk to short-sellers. For longer holding periods, results are both statistically and economically significant. The greatest CARs are in the highest DCR portfolios.

As a robustness check, I also consider stocks that have high days-to-cover ratios and that also exhibit any decrease in shares on loan over a five-day period (as opposed to exhibiting exceptional decreases in shares on loan, as defined earlier). I find that the cumulative abnormal returns for each category are generally no longer positive, and that none is statistically significantly different from zero. This reveals that it is the exceptional nature of short-covering associated with crowded exits that leads to losses for short-sellers.

Summary

To summarise these results, I find that crowded exists are associated with losses to short-sellers that are economically and statistically significant. Stocks with higher short interest, smaller sizes and poorer liquidity are more likely to experience crowded exits.

These findings suggest practical steps that short-sellers can take to mitigate crowded exit risk.

1. Short-sellers should be risk-aware when short-selling less liquid stocks with high days-to-cover ratios.

2. Given the prolonged nature of crowded exits, short-sellers should cover their short positions immediately upon observing exceptional levels of covering by other shorts-sellers in crowded positions. However, such short-covering will in itself exacerbate the crowded exit effect.

Furthermore, there is a time lag between the start of a crowded exit and the release of public data that confirms an exceptional degree of short covering. This highlights the importance to short-sellers of market colour on stock-lending data – amongst other things, such information can allow a trader to stay ahead of the pack in terms of understanding crowded-exit risk.

A warning about using empirical evidence to develop quantitative strategies

It seems rational for investors to take account of published evidence on stock-market anomalies. Indeed, a number of quantitative analysts incorporate empirical evidence on stock market anomalies into their investment processes, in their constant search for out-performance. Various studies suggest that the publication of empirical research influences investor behaviour. For example, Lev and Nissim (2006) study short-selling and the accruals anomaly and find that in recent years institutions have altered their portfolio positions more actively in response to accrual disclosures. Wu (2008) argues that

> short sellers appear to exploit the [post-earnings announcement] drift by increasing (decreasing) shorting immediately following negative (positive) earnings surprises.

Much of this adaptive behaviour is likely to be helpful to the running of markets. We should expect a number of apparent anomalies in markets to be ironed out over time by such behaviour, as traders develop quantitative approaches that are designed to exploit such anomalies. However, some apparently rational adaptive behaviour can lead to surprising, counter-intuitive market outcomes.

Counter-performativity

Recall from earlier that a substantial body of literature shows that heavily shorted stocks perform poorly, as do stocks that experience an increase in borrowing demand. These studies suggest a potential trading strategy for short-sellers: identify heavily shorted stocks (or stocks with increasing borrowing demand) and build short positions in those stocks.

Employing such a strategy, however, changes the market dynamics. Essentially, this strategy involves imitation and so leads to short-positions becoming more crowded. The risk of crowded exits thus increases. This can lead to examples of counter-performativity, a phenomenon described by MacKenzie (2006). In this case, the widespread and plentiful practice of short-selling as envisaged in some asset-pricing models leads not necessarily to a more efficient market as might be expected, but to an increasing number of crowded exits and thus occasions on which stock prices move temporarily *away* from fair value.

" Some apparently rational adaptive behaviour can lead to surprising, counter-intuitive market outcomes. **"**

Ultimately, and surprisingly, greater numbers of arbitrageurs in a market can lead to more examples of mis-pricing, not less, as a result of liquidity problems! This is counter-performativity. Indeed, Irvine (2005) finds that stocks with higher short interest in any given month also have greater return skewness the next month. The distribution of stock returns is influenced by the 'crowdedness' of short positions.

Does it matter if stock prices occasionally diverge from equilibrium levels?

Yes, as the *path of stock returns* is important to investors employing leverage (who are liable to margin calls or subject to loan covenants) and to investment agents using open-ended fund structures (who are subject to the risk of redemption by clients). Even *temporary market imbalances* can lead to unexpected,

> **Greater numbers of arbitrageurs in a market can lead to more examples of mis-pricing, not less, as a result of liquidity problems!**

permanent losses as these classes of investor become unable to hold on to losing positions. Crowded exits can create very real path-dependency problems for short-sellers.

CHAPTER 4

STOP LOSSES

A stop loss is a mechanism whereby a trader attempts to close out a position once the loss on that position exceeds some pre-set threshold. In effect, it is an instruction to buy or sell a defined number of securities once the market price reaches a pre-defined level.

The use of a stop-loss system does not in itself guarantee that the trader limits his loss to the threshold chosen – where liquidity is poor, or where a security gaps in price, it might not be possible to sell the security at the desired price. Nevertheless, some spread-betting firms and investment banks offer guaranteed stops to traders, but as making this offer entails risk, it must be compensated for by means of higher charges or poorer spreads.

Where stop losses are employed, the loss threshold is generally described in either nominal terms (e.g. attempt to sell a security once it has fallen by 7%) or in market relative terms. It can also incorporate adjustments for other factors, such as market volatility. In some cases, portfolio managers describe thresholds in terms of a security's contribution to portfolio returns. For example, a stop loss could be triggered once the loss on a security has reduced fund performance by, say, 50 basis points.

Why use stop losses?

There are four main reasons why one might wish to use stop losses.

1. Client confidence

The first of these is a consequence of the agency relationship between portfolio manager and client. Some clients might associate any large loss within a portfolio with a lack of skill or poor risk control on the part of the portfolio manager. Too many large losses can lead to a loss of confidence in the manager and the eventual termination of the relationship.

Where the portfolio manager anticipates a negative reaction to large losses, he will naturally seek to minimise the risk of large losses ever arising in a portfolio. One way to do this is to use stop losses: the manager attempts to prevent large losses from appearing in the portfolio by crystallising small losses before they can grow too large.

Of course, losses on any single position should not matter as much as overall portfolio returns. However, this is an issue of client confidence rather than mean portfolio returns. Large losses feel uncomfortable to the client and signify failed management decisions. In extreme cases, firms can enter administration or bankruptcy and holdings in these companies have a habit of lingering on portfolio statements for years, until all claims have been settled. Few clients like being reminded of such bad mistakes and managers may choose to use stop losses to reduce the chance of large losses like these appearing in a portfolio.

2. Risk-control mechanisms

A second reason for using stop losses is that traders and portfolio managers employ risk-control mechanisms that lead them to sell stocks in response to losses. For example, a dynamic hedging strategy might seek to limit potential losses in a portfolio to some pre-defined maximum. To do this, the portfolio manager could respond to losses by selling risky assets for cash. Stop losses can be incorporated into such an approach. As asset prices fall, the portfolio is adjusted so that it comprises an increasing proportion of cash. In theory, once losses reach the maximum permitted loss, the portfolio should hold no risky assets at all (just cash).

Unfortunately, there are risks and problems associated with such dynamic hedging strategies, including liquidity constraints and predation risk. As an illustration of these risks, the widespread use of a dynamic option replication technique known as portfolio insurance became increasingly popular in the US equity market during the mid-1980s. It offered to protect equity holders from extreme losses, by selling shares in response to market falls. However, the system ultimately failed to protect portfolio values during the stock market crash of 1987, as it was not possible to sell holdings quickly enough to limit losses to the promised threshold. The system was also believed by some to have exacerbated the market declines, as falls in share prices initially led to further sale orders. Portfolio insurance is now largely discredited in equity markets, although similar approaches can be seen in foreign-exchange markets, where liquidity is much greater. Dynamic hedging in the broadest sense, though, remains of vital importance to options traders.

3. Momentum strategies

A third explanation for the use of stop losses comes from the evidence on price momentum. Jegadeesh and Titman (1993, 2001) and many related studies show that equity momentum strategies (buying winners and selling losers) based on prior performance can generate significantly positive returns for holding periods of three to 12 months. In light of this evidence, traders might expect poorly performing stocks to continue trending lower. Stop losses would thus serve to eliminate these under-performing stocks from portfolios, subject to sufficient liquidity being available. Of course, the possible gains from this approach need to be weighed against direct trading costs and the market impact of the trades.

Loss-realisation aversion

Finally, stop losses can be used to overcome a behavioural pattern known as loss-realisation aversion. The literature on behavioural finance describes a number of investor biases, or apparent divergences from rational behaviour. Amongst these is the tendency for investors to hold on to their losing stocks too long and sell their winners too early.

Shefrin and Statman (1985) called this the disposition effect. They sought to explain it by combining prospect theory (Kahneman and Tversky, 1979) with the notion of mental accounting (Thaler, 1985). Prospect theory suggests that individuals assess outcomes through the change they bring to their current situation (or other reference state) and not through their effect on overall wealth. It also assumes that losses from a reference state are perceived by individuals as larger than positive changes of the same magnitude. Mental accounting provides a framework for the way investors set reference points for the accounts that determine gains and losses. Where an investor creates separate mental accounts for profits in each stock position and applies prospect theory to each account (ignoring interaction effects), a disposition effect would be observed. This is known as a preference-based explanation for the disposition effect.

Psychological explanations could also contribute to this phenomenon – an aversion to realising losses is believed to have its roots in people's desire to avoid feelings of shame, regret and blame from others. Stop losses can be employed to limit this type of bias.

A problem with stop losses

The use of stop losses by traders can represent a form of predictable behaviour. For anyone who knows the positions of the trader, the cost basis of those positions and the stop-loss threshold that is being used, it should be possible to anticipate the trader's actions. This gives rise to predation risk.

Consider the following simple illustration. A stop loss guarantees an order once the market price reaches a certain level. Where the stop-loss order is large and likely to have market impact, there is an incentive for other parties to pre-position their trading books and trigger the stop loss order. This could take the form of a predator short-selling the security in question, draining the market of liquidity and driving the price down in the process. Once the stop loss is triggered, the market experiences yet further demand for liquidity. An unconnected market participant does not know if the latest order is an informed or uninformed trade. Fearing informed trading, many market participants will choose to observe market prices with caution, rather than to step in and correct the imbalance.

Consequently, the price of the asset breaks through the stop-loss threshold. The predator now uses this opportunity to close out his short positions at a profit. The existence of barrier options or knock-out options can present similar opportunities for predators. Where the scale of the position and the knock-out threshold are known, it should be possible to anticipate and precipitate the actions of others for profit.

Effectively, the trader or manager considering the use of stop losses must weigh the benefits of using stop losses with the risk of becoming a victim of predatory trading.

How do stop losses influence portfolio returns?

By employing a stop-loss system, the investor or trader alters the distribution of returns that he is likely to receive. He should expect to obtain fewer extreme negative returns but a greater number of returns at (or around) the stop-loss threshold. The following charts illustrate this effect using simulated stock returns (normally distributed, independent through time with a mean return of 0 and a monthly standard deviation of 8%):

Figure 4.1 - Simulated stock returns without stop-loss rule

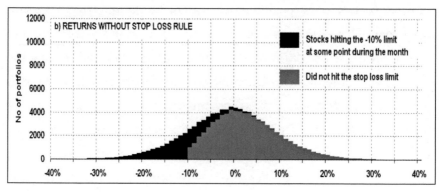

Source: Factset, Macquarie

Figure 4.2 - Simulated stock returns with stop-loss rule

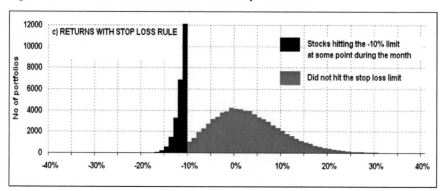

Source: Factset, Macquarie

Figure 4.3 - Changes in the simulated return distribution caused by a stop-loss rule

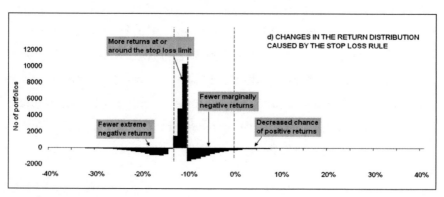

Source: Factset, Macquarie

Figure 4.2 shows that the distribution of returns is modified by the use of a stop-loss rule, with many greater outcomes at around the stop-loss threshold. Figure 4.3 illustrates that when a stop-loss rule is applied, one should expect more returns at or around the stop-loss limit, but also fewer extremely negative, marginally negative or positive returns.

In the real world, stock returns exhibit stock drift and might not be independent through time. They could for example, exhibit momentum or mean-reversion.

The next charts show the impact on monthly returns from the use of stop losses on a universe of around 500 European stocks from 1990 to 2009. Figure 4.4 shows the distribution of monthly returns for this sample, figure 4.5 shows how the distribution is modified without a stop-loss rule with figure 4.6 showing how the distribution is modified by the use of a stop-loss rule. Figure 4.7 shows how stocks perform after breaching the 10% stop loss limit. Finally, figure 4.8 counts the cost of using a stop loss rule.

Figure 4.4 - Distribution of monthly stock returns

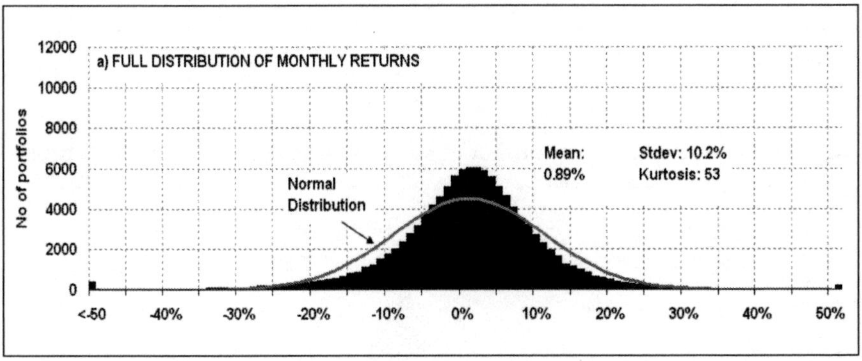

Source: Factset, Macquarie

Figure 4.5 - Stock returns without stop-loss rule

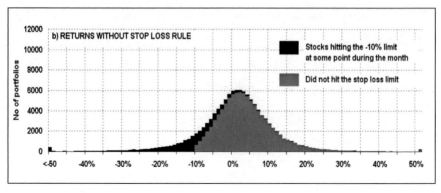

Source: Factset, Macquarie

Figure 4.6 - Stock returns with stop-loss rule

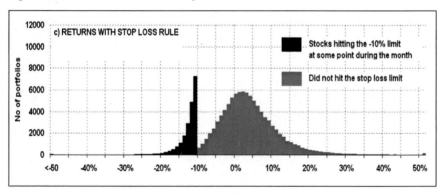

Source: Factset, Macquarie

Figure 4.7 - Conditional distribution of stock returns post stop-loss limit breach

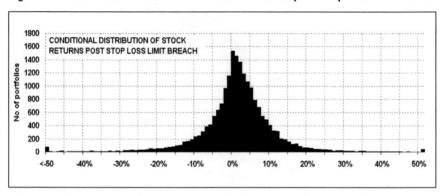

Source: Factset, Macquarie

Figure 4.8 - Cost to portfolio performance from using a stop loss rule

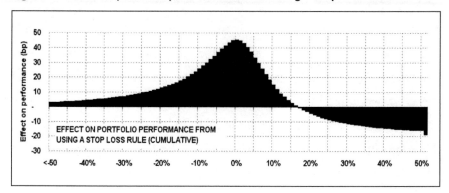

Source: Factset, Macquarie

The net effect of using a -10% absolute loss stop-loss rule with this sample of stocks has been to hurt portfolio returns. In addition, there will be trading costs associated with the use of stop losses. However, the number of stocks breaching an absolute stop-loss limit will vary considerably each month, depending on volatility and the general market direction.

The stop-loss rule can be adjusted to accommodate these two factors. The quantitative research team at Macquarie (2009) tested a variety of stop-loss strategies, including a number of absolute, relative and market/volatility-adjusted thresholds. Where stocks were sold, the proceeds were kept in cash until the end of the month. Conservative assumptions about the sales price achieved were also used. They found that most of these strategies failed to add value in the long-run, although some added value during specific market episodes.

By next assuming that the proceeds of any sales were always re-invested into a general market exchange-traded fund or future, the returns improved and became almost neutral in the long-run. The typical cost attributable to their stop-loss strategies was between 0 and 13 basis points per month for portfolios of the 500 European stocks. Most sector or style sub-portfolios exhibited similar results. Trading costs must also be added to these figures.

Profit taking

By inverting the stop-loss rule so that it becomes a profit-taking rule (i.e. the trader attempts to sell once the gain exceeds some threshold), the results became marginally positive for most trading strategies, at between two and 27 basis points per month, assuming no re-investment of proceeds. When re-investment is included, results improved further. These positive results can be compared to the likely trading costs (and then tested for statistical significance) to evaluate if a trading rule adds value.

US data

Another researcher who has examined the impact of stop losses on portfolio returns and risk is Neil Heywood at Matrix Trading Systems. He began by simulating the activities of an active fund manager by creating portfolios of 25 stocks selected at random from the S&P 500 for the period from 1988 to 2007. The fund manager is then assumed to buy stocks selected at random over time, while maintaining 25 concurrent positions.

Heywood examined the distribution of returns for these portfolios with and without the use of stop losses. By assuming that a position is only closed the day after the threshold is breached, he is incorporating conservative assumptions about the sales price achieved. The following charts apply to active portfolios when there is a stop loss of -15%. Figure 4.9 shows the cumulative performance starting with $1000 for the average active portfolio against the largest 500 US stocks weighted by market capitalisation (benchmark 1) and also weighted equally (benchmark 2).

Figure 4.9 - Cumulative performance for randomly selected portfolios using a -15% stop-loss rule

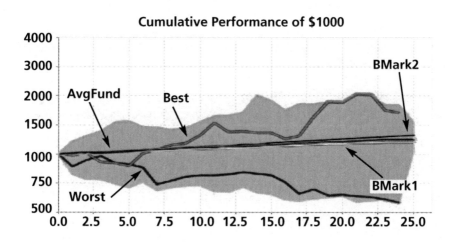

Source: Matrix Trading Systems

Figure 4.10 shows the distribution of monthly returns for the randomly-selected active portfolios:

Figure 4.10 - Distribution of monthly returns for randomly-selected portfolios using a -15% stop-loss rule

Source: Matrix Trading Systems

Table 4.1 shows return, risk and trading activity outcomes for randomly selected active portfolios using no stop loss and then a -7%, -15% and -25% absolute return stop loss rule.

Table 4.1 - Results for applying various stop-loss rules to randomly-selected portfolios of us stocks

	No Stop Loss	-7% Rule	-15% Rule	-25% Rule
Median Return (%)	13.42	11.17	13.26	12.89
Mean Return (%)	11.52	10.39	11.77	11.67
Standard Deviation (%)	11.84	11.26	11.36	11.72
Worst Portfolio Return (%)	-25.95	-24.62	-18.44	-23.59
Number of Trades	50,000	97,000	67,000	57,000

By using the -7% rule, there are many more trades and also lower mean and median returns compared to the portfolios with no stop losses. The use of a -15% stop loss does not appear to hurt portfolio returns, but there is a superior worst-portfolio-return outcome. Outcomes obtained using a -25% stop-loss rule are less attractive than those obtained using a -15% rule.

In aggregate, these results provide no evidence that returns can be boosted through the use of stop losses. They do, however, suggest that stop losses can be used to modify the distribution of returns from a portfolio, affecting its higher moments. Specifically, traders using stop losses present skewness in returns. This weakens the power of some risk-adjusted return measures, such as the Sharpe ratio, when evaluating portfolios or trading books subject to stop-loss rules.

Finally, what happened to stocks after they had stopped out?

Using a six-month window for stocks stopped out after an absolute percentage price fall, Heywood found no discernable difference between the returns from these stocks and those from a randomly-selected portfolio of stocks or a market capitalisation-weighted index of stocks.

> " These results provide no evidence that returns can be boosted through the use of stop losses. "

An aversion to realising losses

Should investors care about the cost basis of their positions and whether it is at a loss or profit?

Where investors are subject to capital gains tax, the answer to this question is clear: we would expect investors to actively harvest tax losses to offset gains and so reduce taxes due in any fiscal year. But where tax is not a concern, we might expect investors to be almost ambivalent between crystallising gains or losses[22].

However, tests reveal that investors prefer to crystallise gains rather than losses. The reluctance of some market participants to realise losses has been the subject of much research. Early empirical studies into the disposition effect and loss aversion involved experiments on students. Later experimental studies were performed using different groups of market practitioners, including retail investors, mutual-fund managers and futures traders.

Odean (1998) tested the disposition effect using customer account data from a discount brokerage house. He found that the propensity to sell a stock declines as losses increase, but also observed selling of losing stocks in December by (US) investors who presumably use the end of the tax year as a self-control mechanism. Retail investors in other countries also show an aversion to realising losses.

---

[22] There could be some bias due to expected mean reversion or momentum effects in asset prices.

What about the professionals?

The behaviour of financial professionals could differ from that of ordinary individuals due to training, regulation and experience. They might be expected to be less prone to the common mistakes or biases exhibited by retail investors.

Locke and Mann (2000) examined professional floor futures traders: they found that traders hold losing trades longer than winning trades and that the average position size for losing trades is larger than that for winning trades. This suggests that the specific group of professionals they studied exhibited a disposition effect. They also found that relative aversion to realising losses is negatively related to current and future relative trading success. In other words, those traders who were less prone to this bias generated better results. Garvey and Murphy (2004) examined data on a US proprietary stock-trading team and found evidence that the traders hold on to losing positions too long and sell their winners too soon. These studies show that professional investors are not immune from an aversion to realising losses.

Coval and Shumway (2001) found evidence of additional intraday risk taking as a response to morning losses amongst professional market makers at the Chicago Board of Trade. Presumably, this represents an attempt by professionals to trade their way out of losses, so as not to end the day in the red. Cici (2005) studied 517 actively managed funds in the USA and found that 37% of the sample funds were affected by the disposition effect. Furthermore, the disposition effect had an economically and statistically significant negative effect on fund performance.

Not everyone is averse to realising losses

Although professional traders as a group exhibit the disposition effect, it is not uniformly exhibited amongst all traders. Brown *et al.* (2002)

examined daily Australian Stock Exchange share data and found that the disposition effect was pervasive across investor classes but that it was less pronounced amongst traders instigating larger investments. Perhaps professional training and expertise can reduce judgmental bias?

Dhar and Zhu (2008) examined the trading records of a brokerage firm to identify individual differences in the disposition bias. They found evidence that wealthier investors, and those in professional occupations, exhibited less trading bias. Furthermore, approximately one fifth of investors in their sample exhibited behaviour opposite to the disposition effect. In summary, there is evidence that the disposition effect can be moderated amongst larger, more experienced investors.

Does this impact asset prices?

Behavioural biases such as loss-realisation aversion could affect the pricing of assets through market microstructure. Some researchers have attempted to understand the impact of this bias on prices by building simple models that include biased or 'irrational' agents[23]. Some of the apparent anomalies found in market behaviour can be explained by assuming the presence of biased investors.

Grinblatt and Han (2004) developed a model of equilibrium asset prices driven by mental accounting and prospect theory, so as to generate outcomes consistent with the empirical evidence on the disposition effect. In the model, the differences between a stock's market price and its aggregate cost basis were positively related to the stock's expected future return, creating a spread between a stock's fundamental value and its equilibrium price, and also an under-reaction to information. Rational arbitrageurs might not be able to eliminate the impact of the disposition

---

[23] For example, Barberis *et al.* (2001) integrated 'loss aversion' into an asset-pricing model and showed that their enhanced model had superior predictive power to alternative models.

effect on equilibrium prices for a variety of reasons, including noise-trader risk and capital constraints. In summary, a pervasive disposition effect amongst investors could lead prices to move away from equilibrium levels and remain mis-priced for some time.

This argument would be open to challenge if it could be shown that the disposition effect reflects only the behaviour of unsophisticated investors who are price followers rather than price setters. An examination into the behaviour of short-sellers with respect to the disposition effect would thus be very illuminating: short-sellers are widely regarded as sophisticated and well-informed market participants. Short-selling is an integral component of arbitrage, a process that in neoclassical finance involves exploiting asset-pricing anomalies, and, in so doing, helps to set asset prices and keep markets efficient.

If it could be shown that short-sellers also suffer from an aversion to realising losses, this would suggest that mis-pricing opportunities could be more common that we might imagine.

Short-sellers and stop losses

Recall that there is no upper limit to the price at which a stock can trade. Consequently, there is no limit, in theory, to the amount of money that a short-seller can lose. This contrasts with the experience of long-only investors, where losses are limited to the amount of capital invested. Exposure to unlimited liability can have catastrophic consequences, including bankruptcy, and is thus an important consideration in risk management.

My interviews with short-sellers reveal that they fear this risk. They also claim to mitigate it through the systematic use of stop losses. I examine this by using my dataset of UK stock-lending and returns data to study the response of short-sellers to losses.

Little formal research has been conducted on short-sellers and their response to losses. The closest academic study has been from Gamboa-Cavazos and Savor (2007), who examined the response of short-sellers to changes in stock prices. Making use of monthly data (157 months) on short interest obtained from NASDAQ, they found that short-sellers covered their positions after stocks rose in price (i.e. after negative returns for short-sellers). The authors also found that stocks bought back by short-sellers did not perform unusually well afterwards, suggesting that such short-covering was not motivated by expected stock returns (i.e. future losses to short-sellers).

The authors argue that short-sellers cannot or will not maintain short positions after suffering losses and put forward two suggestions to explain their results. The first of these is that arbitrageurs have limited capital resources and poorly diversified portfolios, and so cannot bear large losses in individual positions. Their second suggestion is that short-sellers suffer from myopic loss aversion – a behavioural bias that manifests itself in a tendency to shun attractive long-term investments because of an aversion to short-term losses.

Do short-sellers cover in response to book losses?

My study builds on the work of Gamboa-Cavazos and Savor (2007) in two ways. First, I introduce higher frequency data. Short-sellers are renowned for their short time horizons – most studies suggest that the longevity of the average short position can be measured in days rather than months[24]. Monthly data can thus be ill-suited to this type of study and I use daily data to provide greater granularity for understanding the activities of short-sellers.

---

[24] Cohen *et al.* (2007) find that almost half of securities-lending contracts are closed out within two weeks and the median contract length is 11 days. Analysis of securities lending contracts could miss intraday shorting, and so short-selling is likely to be even shorter in duration than these figures suggest.

Secondly, I examine short-covering as a response to accounting losses rather than just stock price increases. I do this by incorporating a technique for estimating the volume-weighted average price at which short positions are initiated. I call this the short-sellers' *cost basis* and compare it to the price at which short covering takes place, to judge whether short-sellers were in profit or loss at the time of covering.

Methodology

To estimate the short-sellers' average cost basis in each stock, I take the first company in the dataset and identify the first occasion on which the number of shares on loan increases. I assume that this increase in shares on loan represents shares borrowed for the purpose of short-selling and estimate the price at which this was done as the average of the opening and closing prices for the stock on that date. This becomes my initial estimate of the cost basis of all short positions for this stock.

This estimate is updated on the next occasion when shares on loan increase. I ignore days when 'shares on loan' are unchanged or decrease, as there are no net new short positions established on these days. With each additional estimate of the price at which shares are shorted for a particular day, I refine my previous estimate of the cost basis of all short sellers by calculating the weighted-average cost basis at which the short positions were established, weighted by the number of shares shorted on each occasion. The estimate is expected to improve over time and I choose a formation period of one year. The whole procedure is repeated for the next stock and so on.

All subsequent analysis on short-seller behaviour is undertaken using data from after the one-year formation period, but the 'estimated cost basis' for each stock is updated every day beyond the formation period.

I start by using a similar approach to that undertaken by Gamboa-Cavazos and Savor, running regressions similar to theirs (but using UK stocks rather than US NASDAQ data). The dependent variable in the regressions is the change in the market capitalisation on loan. The independent variable is change in price and I also add a series of control variables as in the US study.

The explanatory power of this regression is small with an adjusted R^2 of around 1%. The coefficients of the variables are statistically highly significant and the magnitude of the coefficients and of the explanatory power is in line with those found by Gamboa-Cavazos and Savor. This suggests that short-sellers react to price changes in UK stocks in a similar manner to that found on the NASDAQ market.

I next run my own regressions using the percentage of market capitalisation on loan as the dependent variable[25]. I use stock price as an independent variable, but also incorporate an accounting loss variable based on my 'estimated cost basis' for short-sellers. The difference between the estimated cost basis and the share price is found for each occasion that a company's share price rises above the estimated cost basis – this represents the short-sellers' accounting loss.

For ease of interpretation, the absolute values of this series is taken. This loss series enters the regressions along with the price variable. This is done to see whether short-sellers react to the price change or instead to the accounting loss. I also incorporate control variables into the regressions. These are market capitalisation, market-to-book ratio and free-float number of shares (the latter being a proxy for the availability of stock loans).

---

[25] Specifically, the natural logarithm of this variable is taken to mitigate the problem of positive skewness in the distribution.

Specifically, I run the following regressions:

Equation 4.1

```
ln(Market Capitalisation on Loan)_t =
α + θ(lnLoss_t) + β(lnPrice_t) + γ(Market Capitalisation_t) +
δ(Market-to-Book ratio_t) + λ(Free-Float number of Shares_t) + u_t
```

For each regression I take care of the firm effect parametrically by including firm dummies and use clustered by time period standard errors to eliminate the non-fixed time effect. The results of these regressions are shown in Table 4.2.

Table 4.2 - Results using log of market cap on loan as dependent variable

	Panel A - Full Dataset						
	Dependent Variable: Log of Percentage of Market Capitalisation on Loan						
	Log of Price	Market Cap	Market-to-book ratio	Free-Float Number of Shares	Intercept	R-squared	Adjusted R-squared
Coefficients	-0.1001	-0.0001	0.0000	-0.0022	1.4491	0.730	0.728
t-statistics	-1.173	-4.163	-1.961	-1.776	2.970		
p-values	0.241	0.000	0.050	0.076	0.003		

	Panel B - Full Dataset									
	Dependent Variable: Log of Percentage of Market Capitalisation on Loan									
	Log of Loss	Log of Loss_{t-1}	Log of Loss_{t-2}	Log of Price	Market Cap	Market-to-book ratio	Free Float Number of Shares	Intercept	R-squared	Adjusted R-squared
Coefficients	-0.0306			0.1695	-0.0001	0.0000	-0.0006	0.1127	0.769	0.767
t-statistics	-2.586			1.019	-4.344	2.548	-0.343	0.117		
p-values	0.010			0.308	0.000	0.011	0.731	0.907		
Coefficients		-0.0294		0.1646	-0.0001	0.0000	-0.0007	0.1409	0.770	0.768
t-statistics		-2.519		0.996	-4.331	2.540	-0.365	0.147		
p-values		0.012		0.319	0.0000	0.011	0.715	0.883		
Coefficients			-0.0278	0.1588	-0.0001	0.0000	-0.0007	0.1715	0.771	0.768
t-statistics			-2.401	0.965	-4.321	2.537	-0.378	0.179		
p-values			0.016	0.335	0.000	0.011	0.705	0.858		

	Panel C - Top Quintile by Loss						
	Dependent Variable: Log of Percentage of Market Capitalisation on Loan						
	Log of Loss	Log of Price	Market Cap	Market-to-book ratio	FreeFloat Number of Shares	Intercept	R-squared	Adjusted R-squared
Coefficients	-0.0531	0.5462	-0.0001	0.0000	0.0011	-2.522	0.771	0.765
t-statistics	-1.974	1.683	-3.196	6.990	0.368	-1.194		
p-values	0.048	0.092	0.001	0.000	0.721	0.233		

Panel A considers the link between share price as a proxy for loss and the short-sellers' response. The accounting loss variable is introduced in Panel B, first using the specification given in Equation 4.1 and then making use of a lagged loss variable in the second and third regression specifications. Panel C considers solely the top quintile of accounting losses.

Panel A shows a preliminary regression, using log of price but not the accounting loss as an independent variable. The log of price variable is not statistically significant. In the first specification on Panel B, I add in the accounting loss variable and find that the coefficient on the accounting loss variable is negative and statistically significant at the 1% level[26]. At the same time, the coefficient on the price variable remains insignificant. This provides statistically significant evidence that short-sellers cover their positions in response to accounting losses, rather than simply to price increases.

I also examine the relationship between short-interest and lagged accounting losses. In the second and third specifications of Panel B, the loss variable is replaced with a lagged loss variable (a one-day and two-day lag, respectively). The coefficient on the loss variable that is lagged by one day, although statistically significant, is smaller than the coefficient on the non-lagged loss variable and the coefficient on the loss variable lagged by two days is smaller than the coefficient on the loss variable lagged by one day. These results suggest that many short sellers (but not all) react to a loss quickly (within one day). However, as short-sellers are not a homogenous group, some might react to losses only when, for example, accumulated losses lead to margin calls or amount to a certain percentage of capital. Furthermore, individual short-sellers will each have different cost bases.

---

[26] I note the problem of correlation between the two variables, but wish to consider as best as possible the relative importance of the two variables.

Also note that the explanatory power of the regressions described above is high – each adjusted R^2 being around 77%. Running a regression with only the loss variable on the right-hand side of the regression equation reveals a similar adjusted R^2.

I test the robustness of the main regression specification using a restricted sample of the top quintile of the loss series. This subset represents the 'large loss' series. Regression results are shown in Panel C. The coefficient of the loss variable is negative and statistically significant (at the 5% significance level) with the price variable being statistically insignificant. The coefficient of the loss variable from this regression is of greater magnitude than the equivalent coefficient from the regression on the non-restricted sample presented in Panel B. This suggests that short-covering as a response to accounting losses is greater for larger losses.

In summary, the results from Table 4.2 provide significant evidence that short-sellers cover their positions in response to accounting losses, rather than simply to price increases. They respond quickly to losses, and are particularly responsive to large losses.

> The results from Table 4.2 provide significant evidence that short-sellers cover their positions in response to accounting losses, rather than simply to price increases.

Some short-sellers might only cover their positions once losses exceed some pre-defined threshold. To test this, I examined short covering at different levels above the average cost basis of short-sellers (specifically, 2.5% and 5% above the cost basis). I use a similar methodology to that described earlier, except that the loss series is presented in percentage terms relative to price and only losses above 2.5% (or 5%) were recorded. Table 4.3 shows that the coefficient on the loss variable becomes more economically and statistically significant as the percentage loss increases. This provides evidence that there is greater short covering at higher loss thresholds.

Table 4.3 - Dependent variable: market capitalisation on loan

Regression	Independent Variables					Intercept
	Loss	Price	Mkt Cap	Mkt-to-book	Free Float	
Original	-0.082	0.164	-0.000	0.000	-0.004	3.679
	(0.085)	(0.822)	(0.003)	(0.000)	(0.536)	(0.381)
2.50%	-0.223	0.447	-0.000	0.000	-0.004	2.241
	(0.021)	(0.567)	(0.003)	(0.000)	0.529)	(0.618)
5%	-0.348	0.711	-0.000	0.000	-0.006	1.084
	(0.009)	(0.400)	(0.002)	(0.000)	(0.464)	(0.824)

* p-values are in parentheses

Does the use of stop losses hurt short-sellers' returns?

Next, I consider if the returns achieved by short-sellers suffer as a result of using stop-losses. Table 4.4 shows the cumulative abnormal returns for stocks where short covering has taken place after the share price rose above the estimate of the short-sellers' cost basis.

Table 4.4 - Cumulative abnormal returns after short covering

The table reports cumulative abnormal returns (CARs) calculated on an equal-weighted basis for all stocks from days on which two conditions are met: the stock rises above the estimated weighted-average cost basis for short-sellers of that stock; and the number of shares on loan falls that same day and the following day. CARs are calculated for 5, 10 and 30 days after each day on which the two conditions are met.

	5 days	10 days	30 days
Mean	0.0011	0.0023	0.0084
Standard Deviation	0.029	0.043	0.070
Degrees of Freedom	15760	15613	15069
t-stat	4.51	6.62	14.73
Probability (2-tails)	0.0000	0.0000	0.0000

Cumulative abnormal returns for five, ten and 30 days after the day on which the stock price rose above the estimated cost basis are all positive and statistically significant. It thus appears, at first sight, that the short covering spares the short-sellers from further losses.

There is, however, an endogeneity problem associated with such situations: the act of short covering could have market impact, leading in and of itself to stock price increases. It is thus difficult to interpret the above as evidence that short-covering in response to losses prevents further losses to a short-seller. Nevertheless, there is certainly no evidence of an investment performance cost (other than transaction costs) to short-sellers from immediately covering upon falling into loss. From the perspective of a risk manager proposing the use of stop losses, this is an important finding.

Short-sellers as a class do not exhibit an aversion to realising losses, but instead accept their losses or mistakes systematically. Perhaps they are naturally less averse to realising losses than other investors.

Alternatively, those that are free from this bias could prove more successful and gain a greater share of capital, such that short-sellers in aggregate appear not to suffer from loss-realisation aversion.

> " There is certainly no evidence of an investment performance cost (other than transaction costs) to short-sellers from immediately covering upon falling into loss. "

This would tie in with research showing evidence that trading success is negatively related to the degree of loss-realisation aversion. Short-sellers aware of such evidence might respond by adapting their behaviour so as to remove this bias. A self-imposed stop-loss discipline can be used to conquer psychological biases and enforce self-control.

Short-sellers cover in response to book losses. Why?

Although neither legal nor contractual constraints force short-sellers to close their positions at any particular level of loss, there are practical reasons to cover short positions in response to accounting losses. A key reason is that short-sellers face theoretically unlimited losses. By systematically crystallising small losses through the use of stop losses, short-sellers are able to contain this risk.

Portfolio diversification

The desire to maintain portfolio diversification provides another possible explanation for short-covering. For long-investors, winning positions grow in size relative to losing positions and portfolio diversification can be maintained by paring winners. Short-sellers, however, experience the opposite effect: losing positions grow and so these need to be pared to restore portfolio diversification. Short covering upon loss is thus consistent with the use of risk-management

> " Short-sellers in aggregate appear not to suffer from loss-realisation aversion. "

tools to maintain portfolio diversification. Such tools include position limits (i.e. rules governing the maximum permitted size for a portfolio position).

Tax

For taxable investors, there could be tax advantages associated with crystallising losses. However, it is widely believed that short-selling is concentrated amongst funds that generally operate in tax-free, offshore environments. Accordingly, tax reasons are a less likely explanation of the observed results.

Capital constraints

Constrained capital provides another plausible explanation for the tendency of short-sellers to cover in response to accounting losses. Arbitrageurs in practice are generally agents working for owners of capital. They face the risk that ill-informed investors will withdraw their capital in response to accounting losses at the portfolio level, even though the underlying positions might be attractive. This gives arbitrageurs a strong incentive to avoid losses at the portfolio level. By systematically accepting small losses in individual stocks, this reduces the risk of large losses in individual stocks that might cause the overall portfolio to fall into loss.

An additional consideration is that short positions that fall to an accounting loss could require the provision of further margin or collateral (to protect the stock lender or counter-party to a synthetic short position). This could lead to additional strain on the limited capital available to short-sellers. Such strain is mitigated by covering short positions that fall to a loss.

Myopic loss aversion

Could short covering in response to losses be the result of myopic loss aversion – the behavioural bias that manifests itself in a tendency to shun attractive long-term investments because of an aversion to short-term losses? I do not believe so. Consider, first, a long-only environment. An inappropriately short investment horizon and high feedback frequency could lead the investor to close out losing positions and potentially miss out on attractive long-term investments. This is myopic loss aversion.

However, a short position in a risky security generally has a negative expected return. Only with a mis-pricing story will the risky security have a positive expected return, and even then, only in the short-term (because short positions will generally have negative betas). Myopic loss aversion should be irrelevant to situations involving negative long-term expected returns.

Indeed, given that a mis-pricing story is required to make un-hedged short-selling worthwhile, accepting losses appears rational for two reasons: first, if a short-seller believes that the market has mispriced a stock, but finds his short position falling to a loss, this suggests that his original mis-pricing thesis could have been mistaken. It would then make sense to accept the mistake and cover the short position, rather than hold on to a position with a negative expected long-term return.

Second, as a short-seller's position falls to a loss, this suggests that other short-sellers do not observe the same apparent mis-pricing. There is uncertainty about the market-timing decisions of other rational arbitrageurs and thus the timing of any price correction. This is called synchronisation risk. A losing short position suggests heightened synchronisation risk. Abreu and Brunermeier (2002) suggest delayed arbitrage as a response to this problem: this would entail covering and returning to short the stock only as other arbitrageurs start to learn of the over-valuation.

I show that a sophisticated group of traders, strongly associated with price setting, is not averse to realising losses.

In related work, Brown *et al.* (2002) examine the behaviour of investors in Australian stocks across different levels of investor sophistication. They find that the disposition effect is observed for all categories of investor but that "traders instigating larger investments tend to be less, if not entirely unaffected by the disposition bias." Da Silva Rosa *et al.* (2005) observe that (long-only) UK-managed funds do not exhibit the behavioural bias associated with the disposition effect, once size (a proxy for liquidity) and market-to-book (a proxy for value) are taken into account.

Thus, empirical evidence is emerging to show that larger and more sophisticated investors, who are most likely to set prices in markets, do not appear to be biased against realising losses. This is unfortunate news for traders who are seeking systematic mis-pricing opportunities in markets!

Although stop losses appear to be a sensible tool for short-sellers, there is a potential problem arising from their systematic use in response to accounting losses. Specifically, such a use represents a form of predictable behaviour. By knowing (or being able to estimate) the capital strength and cost basis of short-sellers, predators should be able to anticipate short-covering and so position themselves to benefit from the market impact of such trades.

Furthermore, it could be possible for one or more manipulators to *induce* short-covering by placing buy orders when a stock price is *close* to the cost basis of short-sellers. Where the market impact of such trades pushes the stock price above the cost basis of short-sellers, short-covering ensues, placing further upwards pressure on the stock price when liquidity is constrained. The manipulator closes his long position by

" Larger and more sophisticated investors, who are most likely to set prices in markets, do not appear to be biased against realising losses. "

selling stock to a covering short-seller, gaining a profit in the process.

In the next chapter, I examine several forms of manipulation in more detail, including manipulation against short-sellers.

CHAPTER 5

MANIPULATION

The manipulation of securities prices is widely regarded as market abuse, and is consequently considered to be both unethical and illegal[27]. However, markets are not free from manipulation, as evidenced by successful convictions and regulatory fines in various countries over the years. Consequently, traders and investors should gain an understanding of the nature and characteristics of securities manipulation, so as to avoid falling victim to it.

Citigroup

One example of a trading strategy that resulted in regulatory action comes from August 2004, when US bank Citigroup executed a series of trades in the eurozone government-bond market. Implementation of this strategy (nicknamed by Citigroup traders as the "Dr Evil" trade) led to a fine of £13.9 million being imposed by the UK's Financial Services Authority (FSA) in 2005.

According to the *Financial Times* (4 July 2005):

> the bank began by building a long position in cash bonds and going short in bond futures traded on the Eurex exchange. Then, on the morning of August 2, Citigroup bought the equivalent of about 10 per cent of average daily volume in Eurex bund futures that month within 17 minutes. It then sold EUR 12.9 billion in Eurozone government bonds within 18 seconds.

---

[27] One legalised form of price manipulation is the 'stabilisation' of a company's stock price by the sponsoring investment bank around the time of an initial public offering of shares in the company. As the name suggests, this aims to create a relatively stable share price at the outset of trading in new shares.

The FSA stated that Citigroup behaved without

> due regard to the risk and likely consequences of its actions for the efficient and orderly operation of the MTS [bond trading] platform

and that this went against the principles of responsible market conduct.

It is difficult to ever prove that a trading strategy constitutes manipulation, as this requires knowledge of the motivation for the trades. Unless traders leave a trail of indiscreet emails or recorded phone calls, regulators will always need to make judgement calls as to whether or not a pattern of trading constitutes market abuse. Manipulation is thus a difficult practice to uncover. Nevertheless, a series of general principles hold.

Securities manipulation can be sorted into three main types:

1. trade-based

2. information-based and

3. action-based manipulation.

1. Trade-based manipulation

Trade-based manipulation involves the use of trades to earn manipulation profits. In a world where securities prices react principally to the arrival of information, it should not be possible to earn manipulation profits simply through trading. However, if we consider a market eco-system where some players analyse and interpret trading volumes and price trends, then it becomes possible for trade-based manipulation to succeed. A common pattern of trade-based manipulation is often called 'pump and dump' trading.

As an illustration, large trades in a security might be used by a manipulator to build initial positions in that security, but also to create the impression of someone acting on information. The market impact of these trades would tend to push up the price of the security and this constitutes the 'pump' phase of the manipulation. Fictitious trades, including swapping assets back and forth between manipulative parties, can also be used to create an impression of informed trading. These trades attract the attention of other parties, who could interpret them as informed buying. This prompts a revaluation of the stock by the outside parties and precipitates buying, thus luring in outsiders and creating upward pressure on the security price.

In this way, trade-based manipulation can temporarily move security prices away from equilibrium. Trade-based manipulation often involves the exploitation of biases in other investors' behaviour, such as loss aversion or trend-following. For example, as a stock price starts to trend upwards, a price-momentum investor might also buy into the stock, believing that he is simply applying the empirical lesson that positive price momentum is generally associated with high future stock returns. In this case, though, he is simply potential prey for the manipulator. As the stock price climbs and attracts the attention of yet more trend-followers, the manipulator dumps his stock at the higher price, securing a profit.

Eventually, the stock price falls back as no new information emerges to support the inflated price. The manipulative episode thus ends with profits for the manipulator; and losses and disappointment for those lured in by the heightened trading activity and initial stock price momentum.

2. Information-based manipulation

Information-based manipulation involves the use of false accounting or the issuance of false statements and rumours about a security. These could include false rumours about, say, a new oil discovery or a new contract or, on the negative side, problems with cash flow or access to capital.

As an example of alleged information-based manipulation, the *Financial Times* (4 April 2009) reported that "the Australian Securities and Investment Commission is pursuing Mr [Andrew] Forrest and Fortescue Metals for allegedly misleading the stock market over announcements relating to agreements with China Railway Engineering Corp and China Mettalurgical." In particular, the regulator alleged that Fortescue Metals was engaged in

> misleading and deceptive conduct by overstating the substance
> and effect of the agreements.

Information-based manipulation can be used to reinforce pump-and-dump trading, making the manipulation more effective.

Since at least the Great Depression, there has been suspicion amongst some politicians, media commentators and firms that some short-sellers could be the instigators of such forms of manipulations. An alleged example of this from 2008 was the widely-reported claim that short-sellers were manipulating the price of shares in Halifax Bank of Scotland plc (HBOS), using false rumours and short-selling to drive the price lower. Were this true, such behaviour would have constituted information-based manipulation combined with trade-based manipulation. The HBOS rumours led to a formal investigation by the Financial Services Authority, involving a series of interviews with market participants and the examination of phone conversations and trading records. Ultimately, the regulator found no evidence of manipulative behaviour.

3. Action-based manipulation

Action-based manipulation involves the use of some action (e.g. a stock loan recall or a frivolous take-over bid) to move securities prices. Of course, many such actions are not manipulative in nature – it is the motivation behind the actions that determines whether they are manipulative or not.

Later in this chapter I will examine manipulative short squeezes in some detail. These combine action-based manipulation (stock loan recall) with pump-and-dump trade-based manipulation to earn profits at the expense of short-sellers.

Stock pools

Although a single trader can be behind a manipulation, most manipulation schemes brought to the attention of the US SEC (Securities and Exchange Commission) in recent years have generally been undertaken jointly by several parties. The activities of 'stock pools' in the USA in the 1920s – groups of investors who actively traded (and allegedly manipulated prices) in specified securities – are generally believed to be the main reason for the current anti-manipulation laws in the United States and the introduction of the Securities Exchange Act of 1934.

The Senate Banking and Currency Committee (1932 to 1934) concluded that stock pools represented attempts to manipulate the prices of the targeted stocks, although some academic studies dispute that the evidence should have led to this conclusion. For example, Mahoney (1999) examined the trade history of two stock pools to test if price movements in the market were the result of the trades placed by the stock pools and found no evidence of price manipulation by the stock pools. Jiang *et al.* (2005) argue that the size, liquidity and disclosure standards in the stock market at that time "may have been sufficient to protect investors against manipulation". They suggest that enforcement resources should have been targeted on relatively small and illiquid markets, or on discrete segments of the securities markets such as futures markets for commodities and financial instruments that must be delivered (where the supply of the deliverable can be cornered).

There is some empirical evidence that pump-and-dump manipulation can secure profits for manipulators. For example, Khwaja and Mian (2005) examined a 32-month period of aggregated daily trades for each broker and for each stock on the Karachi Stock Exchange (KSE) from December 1998 to August 2001. They found evidence of trade-based pump-and-dump price manipulation:

> When prices are low, colluding brokers trade amongst themselves
> to artificially raise prices and attract positive-feedback traders.
> Once prices have risen, the former exit leaving the latter to suffer
> the ensuing price fall.

The authors argue that several factors that are crucial to successful price manipulation favour brokers over other market participants. First, brokers have lower transaction costs in conducting frequent trading; secondly, they have superior information on prices, trade volumes and traders' expectations; thirdly, they "possess a natural advantage in spreading rumours or false information in the market." Although it is widely believed that large, liquid stocks are less vulnerable to manipulation and abuse than securities that are less liquid, the authors found that manipulation was not confined to small stocks.

Identifying manipulation

Manipulation is characterised by a large abnormal return in the absence of a news announcement, followed by an abnormal return of similar magnitude in the reverse direction, as investors learn that a trade or series of trades was not information-based. By observing patterns such as this in a market, it is possible to test for price manipulation. Additionally, the volatility of a manipulated stock is likely to be greater than that of a similar un-manipulated stock, as a result of the manipulation trades. Evidence of manipulation can also come from so-called nonparametric runs tests: if the returns of a security reflect price manipulation, there should be several continuing days of positive abnormal returns, followed by several days of negative abnormal returns, and the expected number of runs (i.e. blocks of abnormal returns of the same sign) for the period should be lower than expected.

Manipulation around share issues

For some time, there has been suspicion that short-sellers target stocks prior to seasoned equity offerings (SEOs), temporarily driving stock prices lower so as to produce artificial discounts in the price of new shares. The short-sellers would then cover their positions with stock obtained at the issue price, securing a profit in the process. Safieddine and Wilhelm (1996) investigated short-selling activity around SEOs and found that short interest between the date of announcement of an SEO and the offer date is approximately three times the level prior to the announcement. Short interest returned to normal levels after the offer date.

In 1988, the Securities and Exchange Commission adopted Rule 10b-21 as an anti-manipulation measure. The rule prohibited the use of shares purchased at the offer price to cover short positions established after the filing of an SEO registration statement. The level of pre-offer short interest fell after the adoption of this rule. Furthermore, where the rule appeared to be binding, issuing firms suffered smaller discounts.

However, Safieddine and Wilhelm found evidence of regulatory arbitrage where issuing firms had listed options: short-sellers developed synthetic short positions using options, and Rule 10b-21 failed to constrain this activity. Their study provides evidence that short-sellers temporarily drove stock prices lower for their own gain, at the expense of shareholders in firms undertaking SEOs.

In 1997, the SEC relaxed the controls on short-selling around SEOs by replacing Rule 10b-21 with Rule 105 of Regulation M. The new rule prohibited traders from covering short sales made within five days of the offering with shares obtained in the offering.

Henry and Koski (2008) examined a sample of SEOs between 2005 and 2006 and found that: "Around issue dates, higher levels of pre-issue short-selling are significantly related to larger discounts". This observation is consistent with the existence of manipulative trading prior to the issue. High short-selling activity before the issue is also generally associated with a price recovery after the issue, also consistent with manipulation. There was also some evidence that manipulative traders ignored Rule 105.

On 20 June 2007, the SEC strengthened Rule 105 to prohibit anyone who had executed a short sale in the five-day period before an SEO from purchasing shares in the offering, let alone from using the purchase to cover a short position. According to the *Wall Street Journal* (6 December 2006), this change was motivated by the belief that some short-sellers had been avoiding the constraints imposed by the rule.

Henry and Koski found that manipulation around SEOs was confined to non-shelf registrations (there was little evidence of manipulative trading around shelf offerings). This provides valuable information for corporate managers who must choose an SEO registration method.

In late 2008 and early 2009, a series of firms around the world issued new shares to strengthen their balance sheets in response to economic recession. This provides fertile material for investigating possible manipulation around secondary equity issues. Although a definitive study is unlikely to be produced until this episode of SEOs comes to an end, it is simple to examine short-seller activity around individual issues - as a series of case studies. We will now look at two UK utility issues that show interesting price behaviour.

Case study: a placing of stock

The first of these is Scottish and Southern Energy, which announced at 7.00 am on 7 January 2009 its intention to place up to 5% of the issued ordinary share capital with investors. As shown in Figure 5.1 below, the shares fell sharply at the open and in the following hours, under-performing the market on elevated trading volume, as the firm and its advisors negotiated with prospective buyers the price at which the shares should be issued (the 'book build'). The issue price was announced at 3.10 pm that day, along with an announcement that the book building had been successfully completed. The issue price at 1140p was set at approximately 10% below the previous day's closing price. The stock price recovered ground relative to the market over the next few days, matching its pre-issuance relative position within about four days.

Figure 5.1 - Share price, market relative share price and turnover by shares for Scottish and Southern Energy around its share placing in January 2009

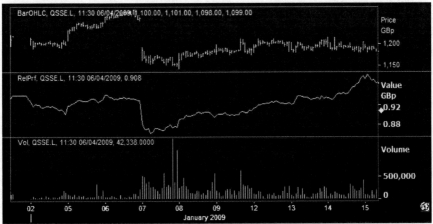

Source: Thomson Reuters

The pattern of trading observed is consistent with that reported by the two academic studies above. The manipulators' strategy would have been to short-sell stock (or sell long positions) on the announcement of the placing. As the share price fell during the book-build period, the sellers and short-sellers could have covered their positions in the market at the new lower market price, or could have requested shares in the placing by expressing interest to the placing institution during the book build. By selling at the open (1174p) and covering in the placing at 1140p, the manipulator makes a 3% intraday profit.

Risks include being unable to cover the position via the placing and having to go into the market at prevailing prices. This risk could be mitigated by learning about the progress of the book-building exercise during the day, via the sponsoring institution. A further risk is of a (positive) fundamental news shock during the book-building process. However, as an integrated power generation and supply utility, the cash flows of SSE are more predictable than those of many other companies, reducing this risk somewhat. Takeover risk would also have to be endured for a few hours. Trading costs and bid-offer spreads would have reduced the profits to some extent, but SSE is a large, liquid stock. Overall, the reward-to-risk ratio looks favourable for this trade. Perhaps only the fear of regulatory action against this type of trading is hard to measure.

Case study: an underwritten rights issue

Another UK utility company that issued shares around this time was Centrica plc. This time, the issuance was in the form of a traditional rights issue, with the price announced at the same time as the rights issue was launched. This mitigates the type of manipulation seen in the SSE case, but still allows for two types of trading strategy: first, the exploitation of any arbitrage opportunities that arise between the ordinary shares and nil-paid rights once the stock trades ex-rights.

Second, the exploitation of the predictable behaviour of any underwriters or sub-underwriters who dynamically hedge their risk positions by short-selling shares in response to share-price declines.

The idea here is that underwriters and sub-underwrites have effectively written out-of-the-money put options on shares in the issuing firm. Where the price falls below the issue price, stock will be 'put' onto the underwriter/sub-underwriters at the issue price and this stock will be difficult to sell without realising a loss. To mitigate this risk, underwriters/sub-underwriters are likely, where permitted, to hedge their exposure by selling shares in response to share-price declines.

This predictable behaviour can be exploited by predators, in the first instance by shorting shares in the issuing firm and driving the price lower. The hedging response can, at its most extreme, create a death-spiral in the share price. This form of predatory trading is sometimes known as the 'crash trade'.

Figure 5.2 shows the activity in Centrica plc shares around its rights issue.

Figure 5.2 - Share price, market relative share price and turnover by shares around the 2008 Centrica rights Issue

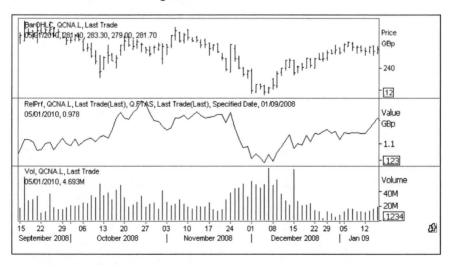

Source: Thomson Reuters

On 31 October 2008 the firm announced a three-for-eight rights issue at 160 pence per share. As can be seen from the chart, its share price performance around this time was relatively stable. However, the stock traded ex-rights on 24 November and from this date, underwriters and sub-underwriters were exposed to the 'crash trade'.

The chart shown in Figure 5.2 is adjusted to reflect the rights received by shareholders on the ex-rights date. It can be seen that the share price started to fall after the ex-rights date. In Figure 5.2, absolute share price is shown in the first panel and relative performance is shown in the second panel. Note also that trading volume (shown on the third panel) was elevated for the rights period.

Rights trading ended on 5 December and the share price reached a trough around this time. New shares began dealing on 15 December. The share price recovered to its pre-rights price over the ensuing month. This is the type of pattern we would expect to see with stock-price manipulation.

Figure 5.3 shows lending activity in Centrica shares around the time of the rights issue.

Figure 5.3 - Stock lending activity around the 2008 Centrica rights Issue

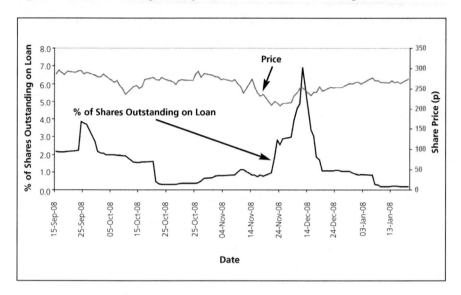

Source: Data Explorers and Thomson Reuters

Observe that short interest in Centrica shares (as shown by the percentage of shares outstanding on loan) increased sharply around the time of the rights issue, indicating heightened activity by stock borrowers (and potentially by short-sellers) around this time. Again, this is what we would expect to find with manipulation around rights issues (although it is in itself not proof of manipulation, as there are other reasons for borrowing shares other than manipulative short-selling[28]).

This pattern of prices and trading volume observed above is consistent with manipulation and the temporary movement of the stock price away from recent equilibrium levels during the period of the rights issue. In this case the share price failed to crash through the rights offer price.

---

[28] Other reasons for additional borrowing include the short-sellers' need to 'manufacture' rights for the lenders of stock. In the above example, this would not fully explain the increase in borrowing that is observed.

Nevertheless, there were opportunities for manipulators to profit at the expense of dynamic hedgers. There were also opportunities for long-term investors to buy stock at favourable prices during the manipulation phase.

Manipulating the shorts

We have a good understanding of manipulation that exploits long investors and, in particular, the predictable behaviour of momentum traders. This includes several theoretical models and also evidence from empirical studies such as Khwaja and Mian (2005). By contrast, very little has been written about manipulation that specifically targets short-sellers as the potential victims.

Short-sellers are particularly vulnerable due to the possibility of stock-loan recall. If a stock loan is recalled and cannot be replaced, the short-seller must cover his position by buying stock in the market. A stock-loan recall thus has the potential to create forced trading, making manipulation more effective. It is the recall mechanism that distinguishes manipulation against short-sellers from manipulation against long-investors. In interviews with short-sellers, a number expressed their fear of becoming a victim of manipulation.

Volkswagen AG

A recent and well-reported case involving alleged manipulation and large losses for short-sellers is provided by activity in the shares and derivatives of Volkswagen AG, a German-based automobile manufacturer, during the autumn of 2008[29]. At the time of writing, this case is the subject of an investigation by BaFin, the German financial

---

[29] See for example, *Financial Times*: 28 October, 5 and 25 November 2008.

regulator. This case has been described by one analyst as "probably the biggest short squeeze in history."[30] I will look at this case study in more detail soon. First, though, it is worth developing an understanding of manipulative short squeezes and the risk these pose to short-sellers.

Short squeezes

In the context of an equity market, a short squeeze is generally described as a situation where a stock loan is recalled and the stock borrower is unable to find an alternative lender. The stock borrower must then purchase shares in the open market to repay the stock loan and to close the position.[31] A short-squeeze is not the same as a crowded exit, but a short squeeze can *become* a crowded exit under some circumstances.

Where a short-squeeze occurs in a highly liquid stock, the short-seller simply buys stock in the market to cover his position, and these purchases would have little market impact. The short-seller bears trading costs and would also suffer an opportunity cost if the stock price fell subsequent to the short covering. A short squeeze in a highly liquid stock is thus an inconvenience, results in minor trading costs and could have an opportunity cost.

By contrast, consider a short squeeze where a stock's liquidity was poor in the context of the scale of the recall. Short covering would have market impact, imposing losses on the short-seller. In an extreme case, other short-sellers might observe the increase in trading volume and

---

[30] This quote is from Max Warburton, analyst at Sanford Bernstein, as reported by Richard Milne of the London *Financial Times* (see *Financial Times*, 28 October 2008).

[31] Dechow *et al.* (2001) provide this definition. A similar definition is offered by Duffie *et al.* (2002): "The lender may opt out of a continuing lending arrangement by issuing a recall notice, in which case the borrower must return the stock. ...In some cases, called 'short squeezes', the borrower (or its broker) is unable to locate lendable shares and is 'bought in', that is, must buy the stock outright. If the borrower fails to deliver the security in standard settlement time, the lender itself may buy it, using the cash collateral."

stock price, and begin to cover their own positions. Thus, a short squeeze could result in a crowded exit if the market impact of the initial short covering is large, or if the squeeze precipitates much additional short covering relative to the stock's liquidity.

It is possible to divide short squeezes into two types: 'manipulative' and 'non-manipulative' short squeezes. A non-manipulative short squeeze occurs naturally when a stock lender recalls his stock (say, to settle a stock sale) and the short-seller is unable to replace his stock loan, due to limited supply. A manipulative short squeeze, however, is associated with deliberate recall by the stock lender as part of a broader manipulation strategy.

Consider the situation where a manipulator owns shares in a company and those shares are on loan to a short-seller. The manipulator wishes to pump up the share price and so buys *additional* shares in the company, demanding liquidity from the market. Simultaneously, he recalls the stock that is on loan. If unable to locate new stock to borrow, the short-seller must cover his position by buying stock in the open market. The market impact of these purchases places further upwards pressure on the stock price. The short-seller suffers a loss as he covers his position at a price above the initial, undisturbed share price. Finally, the manipulator dumps his shares at the new, higher share price. In so doing, he secures a profit and completes the manipulation process.

Figure 5.4 - Illustrates the relationship between 'crowded positions', 'crowded exits', 'short squeezes' and 'manipulative short squeezes'

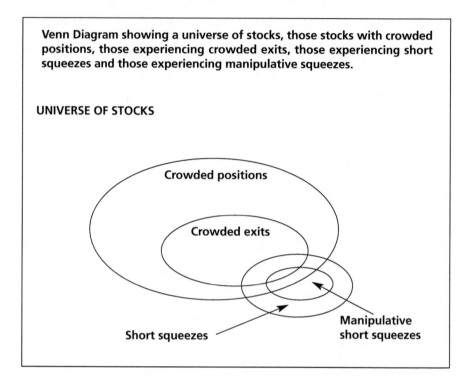

Venn Diagram showing a universe of stocks, those stocks with crowded positions, those experiencing crowded exits, those experiencing short squeezes and those experiencing manipulative squeezes.

UNIVERSE OF STOCKS

Crowded positions

Crowded exits

Short squeezes

Manipulative short squeezes

Manipulative short squeezes can be seen to be a subset of short squeezes. Furthermore, some manipulative short squeezes belong to the set of crowded exits.

Short-sellers thus face the risk of becoming victims of manipulation and it would be helpful to understand this risk better. For instance:

- How often do short-sellers become the victim of manipulative short squeezes?

- What types of stock are associated with manipulative short squeezes?

- How much do short-sellers lose when they do become victims?

The answers to these questions are largely unknown – stock-loan recalls and short squeezes are frequently described in academic work, but are rarely researched further. One exception is D'Avolio (2002), who investigates stock-loan recalls and finds that it can be difficult to re-borrow stock after a recall. He finds that 2% of stocks on loan are recalled during an average month, and that it takes a mean of 23 days (and a median of nine days) to replace a recalled stock loan. Under existing regulations (e.g. Regulation SHO in the USA), a short-seller would be unable to hold on to a short position for such extended periods of time without a stock loan. This suggests that the recall of a stock loan typically leads to the need to cover the short position.

Accordingly, a manipulator can, under certain circumstances, use a stock loan recall to induce short-covering. The short covering represents a forced trade. As we saw in Chapter 2, forced trading can be exploited by predators. In this case, by recalling stock that is hard to borrow, the predator can *create* a situation that leads to the forced trade.

For manipulators, information about the stock positions and capital strength of short-sellers can be valuable. Such information would allow the manipulator to better understand the ecology of the stock market. By knowing the price at which a short-seller established his short position, the manipulator also knows at what stock price the short-seller would experience a loss; by knowing the capital strength of the short-seller, the manipulator better understands the short-seller's ability to meet margin calls and thus to maintain losing positions. Such information allows the manipulator to gain a better understanding of when manipulation is likely to succeed.

Manipulators can infer much valuable 'ecological' information from publicly-disclosed data on stock lending, trading volume, stock returns and share holdings. However, market participants with access to proprietary client trade flows hold a further advantage, as they can obtain granular data in a timely fashion. Such proprietary information would be very valuable to a manipulator, and firms with access to this type of data normally establish policies to disallow its use for manipulative purposes.

Nevertheless, De Long *et al.* (1990) suggest that such information is commonly used by traders within investment banks.[32] Trading and risk arbitrage are social phenomena, performed amongst a community of traders largely known to one another. 'Well-connected' traders, who receive rumours or information about the activities of other traders, are at an advantage to those without such information. If it were not illegal and unethical, it would certainly be rational for a trader to obtain and use such information, given the theoretical foundations for generating abnormal returns via manipulation and predatory trading.

Writing in the *Financial Analysts Journal*, Jacobs and Levy (2007) assert that the *fear* of short squeezes deters some short-sellers, but that this fear is largely unfounded as short squeezes are rare events and confined to illiquid stocks. The authors do not, however, provide any evidence to back up this claim.

In the next section I aim to determine the frequency and nature of manipulative short squeezes, the losses that short-sellers suffer and the type of stocks affected. I use the panel of data that I described in Chapter 3 to examine the evidence.

---

[32] De Long *et al.* (1990) state: "Another, perhaps more common example of destabilizing rational speculation would be front-running by investment banks. Investment banks and brokers familiar with the customer order flow have perhaps the best information about future levels of demand."

Characteristics of a manipulative short squeeze

A manipulative short squeeze follows the general pattern of pump-and-dump trading. In addition, though, it involves the recall of a stock loan. A manipulative short squeeze thus combines two types of manipulation: trade-based manipulation (pump and dump) and action-based manipulation (stock-loan recall). I describe the full manipulative short-squeeze process as 'pump, squeeze and dump'.

There are considerable practical challenges to researching manipulative short squeezes. It is difficult to differentiate between informed trading and trade-based manipulation just by examining short-run trading data. We simply do not know the motivation for the trading that we can observe. Thus, it will be difficult to use data to distinguish between a manipulative short squeeze and informed trading.

There is a further problem: stock-lending markets are decentralised and there is no legal requirement to report a stock-loan recall. Thus, there is no publicly available data that explicitly identifies stock loan recalls and it will not be possible to affirmatively identify a manipulative short squeeze from public data on stock lending or short-selling. It will only possible to *infer* stock-loan recalls from patterns in the data. Even if we had private data that revealed stock loan recalls, the motivation behind each recall would remain unknown. As manipulation is deemed illegal in most markets, we should expect it to be disguised. Direct questioning of a manipulator is unlikely to reveal the true motivation for a manipulative trade or action.

In light of the practical difficulties in identifying manipulative short squeezes, it is little surprise that this topic is under-researched and poorly understood.

To investigate manipulative short squeezes in more detail, it will be necessary to overcome these problems. To do this, I define a pattern of market data with respect to stock returns and total shares on loan that is *consistent* with a manipulative short squeeze. I call such an event an 'apparent manipulative short squeeze'. I describe a set of rules for identifying apparent manipulative short squeezes in the methodology section.

It is, of course, possible that patterns in the stock and stock loan market that are consistent with manipulative short squeezes could simply be the result of noise. Consequently, my group of apparent manipulative short squeezes could exceed the actual occurrence of manipulative short squeezes. Although this appears to be a limitation of the research, one of the purposes of this study is to examine the frequency of manipulative short squeezes. If I find that *apparent* manipulative short squeezes are uncommon, this suggests that *actual* manipulative short squeezes are also uncommon.

Definition of an 'apparent manipulative short squeeze'

I define an 'apparent manipulative short squeeze' as any situation in which all of the following occur: the stock price rises 'exceptionally' over some given time period (the 'pump' phase), followed by a fall in the number of shares on loan as lent stock is recalled (the 'squeeze' phase); subsequently, the stock price reverts towards the original, undisturbed level (the 'dump' phase) as the manipulators sell their shares at the higher price, thus securing a profit for themselves.

Furthermore, these events should not coincide with any regulatory news announcements (these might include trading statements, corporate results, announcement of share buybacks, change of directors etc).

This latter requirement avoids the confounding of a manipulative short squeeze with reaction to new, public, company-specific information. By requiring that an exceptional price rise is followed by a price reversal, I am able to separate a manipulative short squeeze from informed trading upon private information. We would not expect a price reversal when the stock price reacts to new private information.

Separating apparent manipulative short squeezes from noise trading

The remaining difficulty is in separating an apparent manipulative short squeeze from noise trading. Noise trading could also lead to a rise in share price followed by a reversal. I attempt to separate the two phenomena as follows: first, by requiring that the initial share price rise is exceptional. Noise trading is associated with trading by uninformed market participants. Traditional asset-pricing theories generally consider the actions of noise traders to be uncorrelated amongst one another. Under such a framework, their market impact is less likely to be large, and so any stock-price reaction to noise trading is likely to be limited and thus excluded by this criterion.

Secondly, I require that shares on loan fall after the stock-price rise. Whereas loan recalls mechanically create pressure for a reduction in shares on loan, there is no similar mechanical link between price changes due to noise and shares on loan. Nevertheless, it is not possible to fully disentangle the two phenomena and this becomes a limitation of the work that follows.

Next, I must define an 'exceptional' rise in stock price. I choose to define an exceptional rise in stock price as one that is large relative to the volatility of returns for that stock.

Furthermore, I measure price changes over a three-day period. A three-day period is chosen because, in the UK, stock-loan recalls are settled in the same way as stock purchases, meaning that borrowers have three working days to return the stock[33]. In particular, once a stock loan is recalled, a borrower who has shorted stock has three options: first, he could successfully find replacement stock; secondly, if unable to successfully find replacement stock, he could delay the return of the stock loan for up to three days in the hope of finding an alternative source of borrowing in this time; thirdly, he could cover his short position immediately and return the stock loan.

Thus, even where the pump phase coincides with a stock-loan recall, it could take up to three days before the short-seller covers his position. For this reason, I measure the pump phase over three days.

For each firm day, I measure the standard deviation of returns for the preceding 60 days. 60 days is sufficiently long to allow for a meaningful estimate of stock-return volatility, but also short enough to be current. By measuring return volatility in this way for each firm day, I take account of the fact that volatility varies over time. I regard an exceptional stock-price increase to be one where the stock price rises over any three-day period by at least 2.5 times the standard deviation of daily returns for that stock. Assuming an approximately normal distribution of stock returns, this method would generally isolate situations that fall within the top percentile of stock-price changes.

By setting this specific definition, I establish an upper count to the frequency of 'apparent manipulative short squeezes'. I also undertake robustness tests using different thresholds later.

After receiving an order to return a stock loan, I expect a short-seller will search for alternative sources of borrowing. If a replacement loan

---

[33] A typical stock-lending agreement in the UK requires the return of stock within three days of recall. Failure to return recalled stock within this time entitles the lender to claim costs from the borrower, and to serve a written notice of 'Event of Default'. The serving of such a notice can have repercussions for the borrower with respect to other counter-parties.

is found, the short position need not be covered. However, the UK lending market is decentralised and so finding replacement shares can take time. D'Avolio (2002) observes for his sample of US stocks that when loans are recalled, there is usually no immediate replacement available. Since in the UK it takes three days to deliver purchased stock under standard settlement arrangements, some short-sellers might be expected to cover immediately upon loan recall.

However, there is another group of borrowers who might prefer to delay covering their positions and look for replacement loans in subsequent days. If unsuccessful and eventually forced to cover, they will have to pay a premium for the delivery of stock to be made in one or two, rather than three, days. Moreover, uninformed traders might start taking long positions around the same time, believing that the buyers they observe are informed market participants.

On the whole, there is likely to be a lot of noise in the stock price on the days immediately after the recall, but it is realistic to expect that the initial stock-price rise will start to reverse by the third day after the stock-loan recall. I define the event date (day 0) as the first day following the exceptional rise in share price on which the number of shares on loan falls.

I ensure that there are no regulatory news service announcements from five days prior to the event date until ten days after the event date. Thus, the observed patterns are not the result of reactions to new, public information.

It is not clear over what time period the stock-price reversal should take place. Most theoretical models of predatory trading or price manipulation assume complete price reversal, but use notional time periods. Thus, I expect complete price reversal over some unknown time period. If I over-estimate the time period, I should expect to observe complete price reversal, but am more likely to introduce confounding influences such as a change in company or economic fundamentals. By underestimating the time period, I would expect to see partial price reversal only.

Without a good theory on the time taken for a stock price to revert fully to its recent equilibrium level, I prefer to identify partial reversal over a limited time period, as this reduces the risk of confounding factors contaminating the study. I report cases with a price reversal of at least 70% over a ten-day period following the event date.

Estimating abnormal returns around apparent manipulative short squeezes

Having identified a number of apparent manipulative short-squeezes, I then estimate abnormal returns for the stocks involved[34]. Due to the small number of observations in each sample and the presence of some large-cap stocks, I prefer to use equally-weighted returns when aggregating the results.

I estimate abnormal returns for each of the three phases associated with an apparent manipulative short squeeze.

1. Phase 1 (the 'pump' phase): lasts for three days, from day -3 to -1

2. Phase 2 (the 'squeeze' phase): also lasts for three days, from day 0 to day 2

3. Phase 3 (the 'dump' phase): lasts for ten days, from day 3 to day 12

Figure 5.5 illustrates these three phases in the form of a timeline.

---

[34] I use the CAPM (capital asset-pricing model) model to estimate abnormal returns and employ a one-year formation period to estimate betas for this model.

Figure 5.5 - Timeline representing the three phases of an apparent manipulative short squeeze

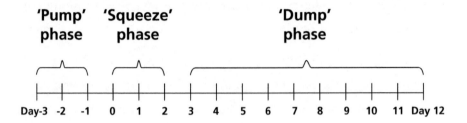

The final step is to calculate how much short-sellers lose as a result of the manipulation. I calculate average cumulative abnormal returns from the start of the pump phase to the end of the squeeze phase (i.e. from day -3 to day 2). By this time, short covering is expected to have been completed and the short-seller should no longer be exposed to stock-price movements.

However, during the pump phase (i.e. day -3 to day -1) short-sellers are highly likely to have experienced negative abnormal returns, because stock prices were increasing by definition. Including this interval in the analysis might result in a biased outcome. As a solution to this problem, I adopt an alternative approach that starts to measure cumulative abnormal returns from event day (day 0) until the end of the squeeze phase (day 2). I then test if these returns are statistically significantly different from 0.

Results

I find 36 instances where a stock price rises exceptionally, then shares on loan decrease, followed by a stock-price reversal, in accordance with my definitions above. Of these 36, some could represent noise rather than manipulation. To consider how many might be due to noise, I run a mirror-image test on the full dataset to identify the number of times the *opposite* pattern in market prices and shares on loan occurs (i.e. significant decreases in share price, followed by a rise in the number of shares on loan, followed by a reversal in share price). This mirror-image pattern would not be associated with manipulation against short-sellers, but would be expected to be subject to a similar degree of noise.

If manipulative short squeezes do not occur in the market at all, one would expect the mirror-image test to produce approximately the same number of observations as the apparent manipulative short squeeze test. I observe 25 mirror-image test events, compared to 36 apparent manipulative short squeezes. This lower number of mirror-image test events is consistent with the notion that some, but not all, apparent manipulative short squeezes are simply the result of noise.

Of the 36 apparent manipulative short squeezes identified above, 16 are associated with regulatory news announcements. I eliminate these, as it is not possible to distinguish between a reaction to a news release and a manipulative short squeeze. This leaves 20 instances matching my definition of an apparent manipulative short squeeze and free from the confounding effects of any regulatory news releases.

This is a small number of instances to observe over 979 days for between 350 and 681 stocks. The proportion of observations that follow the whole pattern is very small, providing evidence that apparent manipulative short squeezes are rare events.

I examine the abnormal returns for stocks involved in apparent manipulative short squeezes for each day during the manipulation process (days -3 to 12). I group the companies into portfolios and show the average abnormal return for each day in Figure 5.6. The two dotted lines are the upper and lower values for the 95% confidence intervals.

The greatest magnitudes for the daily abnormal returns are observed during the pump phase and on the event day. The confidence intervals show that these returns are statistically significantly different from zero.

Figure 5.6 - Abnormal returns around apparent manipulative short squeezes

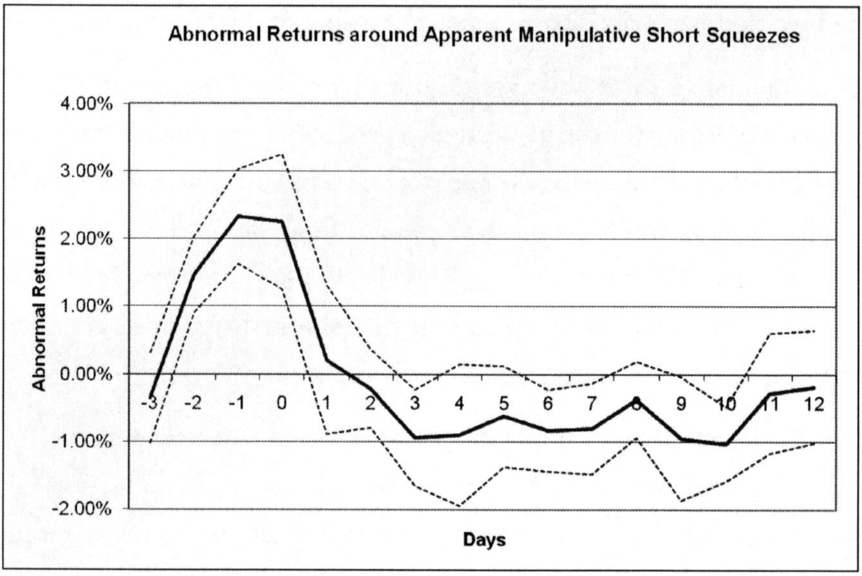

To consider the potential losses to short-sellers, I estimate the cumulative abnormal returns associated with the pump and squeeze phases of the apparent manipulative short squeezes. Figure 5.7 presents the results.

Figure 5.7 - Cumulative abnormal returns by day (starting from day -3)

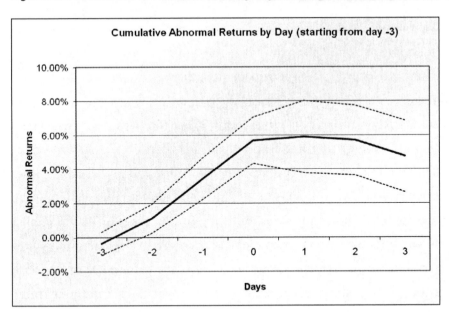

There are significant positive abnormal returns of 3.45% in the first phase (days -3 to -1) and significant positive abnormal returns of 2.26% in the second phase (days 0 to 2). These positive abnormal returns are followed by significant reversals in the third phase. The above results indicate significant losses for short-sellers around apparent manipulative short squeezes.

The charts above show *averages* for a portfolio of stocks subject to apparent manipulative short squeezes. Within these portfolios, the maximum loss a short-seller would have suffered from any *individual* stock was 8.16% in phase one and 13.74% in phase two. Of course, a trader would normally hold a number of short positions at any time and stocks subject to manipulative short squeezes are likely to form only a subset of these short positions. When considered in this broader context, even the largest abnormal returns observed above are likely to be of only moderate economic significance.

Robustness checks

The above results depend on the initial definition that I gave for an apparent manipulative short squeeze. As a robustness check, I also examined 'phase one' stock price rises that represent two (and three) standard deviation changes in stock price, as opposed to the original 2.5 standard deviations. I also filtered for 'phase three' stock price reversals that are both greater and lower than the criterion of a 70% reversal. There is likely to be more noise in the results obtained using looser criteria and unsurprisingly I obtain a greater number of 'apparent manipulative short squeezes' by using looser criteria (and a smaller number of observations with the stricter criteria). The magnitude of the mean abnormal returns varies inversely with the number of apparent manipulative short squeezes that pass through the defining filter. Nevertheless, the sensitivity of the results to the changes in definition is not extreme. As I vary the definitions around my starting point, I continue to find that apparent manipulative short squeezes are rare events that are statistically significant but of limited or moderate economic significance.

An alternative approach

I also investigated an entirely different means of detecting a manipulative short squeeze. The manipulation process comprises stock-loan recall, the removal of the recalled stock from the pool of stock available to borrow, and an attempt by the original stock borrower to replace the recalled stock. As such, a manipulative short squeeze should be associated with a reduction in shares on loan for the stock concerned. Also, there should be an increase (or at least no reduction) in stock-lending fee, as demand for borrowing stock is unchanged but the supply of stock available for borrowing has fallen. The stock-loan-utilisation rate (i.e. the proportion of shares available for borrowing that are actually borrowed) should increase as the victim of the recall seeks to replace his loan from the remaining pool of stock available for borrowing.

I measured the abnormal returns for stocks around periods when these three conditions held, but found no significant evidence that abnormal returns differed from zero. I refined the above analysis to focus on situations where the stock-loan utilisation rate was in the top 5% of all such observations[35]. Manipulative short squeezes are more likely to occur in stocks with high utilisation rates, as a stock-lending agent is more likely to pass a recall on to the stock borrower when the utilisation rate is high (i.e. the loan is harder to replace). Results now became statistically significant prior to the squeeze phase, but were of limited economic significance.

Characteristics of stock subject to apparent manipulative short squeezes

I also examine the characteristics of stocks around the time of apparent manipulative short squeezes. Manipulation is generally believed to be associated with securities that have smaller size, poorer liquidity, elevated volatility of stock returns and elevated trading volume.

I find that the majority of stocks have market capitalisations of less than one-fifth of the market average. This provides some support for the argument that smaller companies are more vulnerable to manipulative short squeezes. However, a small number of large-cap stock observations increase the portfolio mean market capitalisation, so that it is above the market average.

---

[35] Thanks to Will Duff-Gordon at Data Explorers Ltd for this idea.

I obtain two proxies for liquidity in those stocks subject to apparent manipulative short squeezes.

- The first of these is the number of days of normal trading volume that it would take a short-seller to cover his position (the **days-to-cover ratio** or 'DCR'). A stock with a high DCR is deemed to be less liquid (from a short-seller's perspective) than a comparable stock with a lower ratio. The portfolio mean DCR at day 0 is 103.4% of its three-month average, but this is not statistically significant. The percentage of shares on loan is not elevated for stocks subject to apparent manipulative short squeezes.

- Secondly, I compare the **free-float number of shares** for each stock ` with that of the average stock on the event day. The majority of stocks have a free-float value of shares less than one-fifth the market average. This supports the view that less liquid stocks are more vulnerable to manipulation.

The stock-price volatility of a manipulated stock is expected to be greater than that of a similar un-manipulated stock. I measure the volatility of stock returns for each company that is subject to an apparent manipulative short squeeze around the event date. For each of these firm days, volatility is calculated as the standard deviation of returns for the 20 preceding days.[36] I then compare the stock volatility measure to the year's average for that firm. At day 0, for example, this measure reads 103.2% of the annual average – slightly above average but not statistically significant.

---

[36] The number of days needs to be as small as possible to grasp the changes in volatility that we expect to see around the manipulative short squeeze. Nevertheless, this number still has to be sufficient to calculate reliable standard deviations. I choose 20 days as a compromise between these two requirements.

For each stock subject to an apparent manipulative short squeeze, I record trading volume for the five days preceding the start of the manipulation process and compare this to the three month average trading volume for the stock. The mean trading volume is elevated prior to an apparent manipulative short squeeze at 123.6% of its three month average, but again this result is not statistically significant.

In conclusion, there is weak support for the notion that apparent manipulative short squeezes are associated with stocks that have smaller market capitalisation and free float, elevated trading volume and reduced liquidity.

Could knowledge of these characteristics assist in predicting manipulative short squeezes?

To see if this is possible, I identify all instances in the dataset where the market cap and free-float value of a company are below the market average and where the stock's DCR and turnover are above their 60-day average. Each of these events would, in effect, be a red flag alerting the short-seller to the possibility of a manipulative short squeeze. If a stock has more than one day when it satisfies these conditions, I treat every such occurrence as a separate event. In total, I find 12,909 firm days satisfying the conditions described above. However, there is on average *no* price response around these occurrences. This suggests that it is difficult to predict a manipulative short squeeze based strictly on these size, trading volume and liquidity criteria, as many false positives will emerge.

Jacobs and Levy (2007) argue that if a security does become subject to a short squeeze then a reduction in the supply of loanable stock is usually signalled by a decline in the rebate rate offered by prime brokers or by warnings from the prime brokers, so the position can be scaled back or covered in advance of any demand that borrowed stock be returned. According to this argument, short squeezes are rare and can largely be predicted. As such, they pose little threat to short-sellers.

I test this argument on my sample of apparent manipulative short squeezes by studying stock-loan utilisation rates (a measure of the proportion of available stock to borrow that is indeed borrowed) and stock-loan fees around the time of the apparent short squeezes. I find no evidence that utilisation rates and stock-lending fees rise around the time of the apparent manipulative short squeezes. This is not consistent with the argument put forward by Jacobs and Levy. I attribute this to the fact that my dataset considers the larger UK stocks (market capitalisations of £25 million and above) where the availability of stock to borrow is relatively high. For smaller stocks, loan availability is more likely to be problematic.

My findings indicate that it is difficult to predict a manipulative short squeeze using publicly-available information. It is perhaps this characteristic – that these are unpredictable events that can have economic impact – that has led to the fear of manipulative short squeezes amongst practitioners.

A short-seller who fears manipulative short squeezes can take practical steps to mitigate this risk. Short-sellers can pay additional fees to borrow on a term basis (i.e. for a fixed period of time) rather than on a call basis (i.e. with repayment of the loan on demand). However, term loans are not common, despite their ability to reduce the risk of a short squeeze. This might be due to legal and/or liquidity constraints on a stock lender, or the costs associated with term loans.

Another means of managing the risk of a short squeeze is the possibility of borrowing more shares than required for short-selling. Excess borrowing results in greater stock-lending costs, but creates a buffer: if only a portion of the borrowed shares are recalled, the excess shares are delivered first to the lender, so that immediate short covering is not

> " My findings indicate that it is difficult to predict a manipulative short squeeze using publicly-available information. "

required. Both of these techniques incur a cost but reduce the risk of becoming the victim of a manipulative short squeeze.

The Volkswagen case

The evidence emerging from my dataset showed that manipulative short squeezes were rare events that had limited economic significance. These findings were roughly in accord with the received wisdom on the subject, as summarised by Jacobs and Levy. But no sooner had I completed this research, than a possible counter-example emerged in a different country and at a different time from my study. This exceptional case involved activity in the shares and derivatives of Volkswagen AG, during the autumn of 2008.

Volkswagen was a large-cap company (one of Germany's largest companies by market capitalisation) but had a limited free float. By September, 2008, rival car manufacturer Porsche AG had a publicly declared stake of 42.6% of the ordinary shares in Volkswagen AG. A further 20.2% of the ordinary shares were owned by the Lower Saxony Land Government – a long-term stock-holder. Thus, the free float in Volkswagen ordinary shares was only 37.2% of the firm's market capitalisation.

Over a period of time, the relationship between the price of the Volkswagen's ordinary shares and its preference shares had started to diverge from its long-term average, and risk-arbitrageurs had increased their short positions in the ordinary shares of the company. By 24 September 2008, 16.39% of Volkswagen stock was on loan. Unbeknownst to the risk-arbitrageurs, Porsche AG had purchased a cash-settled option position over a further 31.5% of the company. Porsche was not required to disclose its ownership of this option position under German financial regulations.

If this cash-settled option could be converted into Volkswagen stock by agreement with the counterparties to the transaction, then Porsche would have effective control over 74.1% of the company. Thus, the effective free-float in Volkswagen shares would not have been 37.2%, but instead 5.7% of market capitalisation – less than the short-sellers' aggregate position. Conditional on this conversion of the cash-covered option, short-sellers had effectively become cornered – but were unaware of this! As Porsche released news of its option position to the market, short-sellers realised that they were vulnerable to recall risk and margin calls. The price of Volkswagen shares rose sharply (by approximately 400% in a matter of days).

The exact cause(s) of this price rise have yet to be fully understood. Possible reasons include pre-emptive short-covering, forced short-covering after stock-loan recall and dynamic hedging by the counter-parties to Porsche's cash-settled options. Volkswagen briefly became the world's most valuable company by market capitalisation, despite deteriorating fundamentals for car manufacturers at the time. Figure 5.8 shows the stock price, trading volume and relative stock performance for Volkswagen around this time.

Figure 5.8 - Market data for Volkswagen AG shares (autumn 2008)

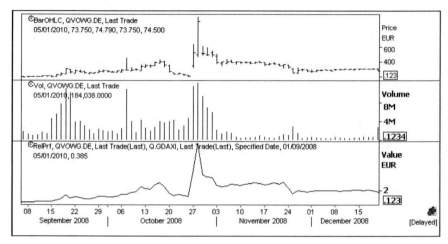

Source: Thomson Reuters

The charts above show a series of shocks to the Volkswagen share price, beginning in mid-September with a second shock in mid-October and with a final blowout to the share price in late October. This is akin to an earthquake with aftershocks, where the aftershocks prove more deadly than the original earthquake.

Porsche later announced that it would sell shares in Volkswagen to facilitate an orderly covering of short positions. By November, Porsche revealed that it had made a profit of €6.8 billion through its trading of options in Volkswagen stock. A series of short-sellers announced large losses and the general suspicion arose that the short-sellers' had become the victims of stock manipulation.

As a result of these suspicions, the German financial regulator initiated an investigation into trading in Volkswagen shares and options. This investigation remains ongoing at the time of writing, but might help to answer questions about the exact nature of Porsche's cash-settled option; about the actions of counter-parties to this option, about the availability of stock loans and any loan recalls around the time of the share-price rise.

Figure 5.9 shows the percentage of shares on loan, the stock-loan utilisation rate and the average stock-loan fee for Volkswagen AG ordinary shares around the event day, day 0, defined as the first day on which shares on loan falls after an exceptional three day share price rise (25 September 2008 in this case).

Figure 5.9 - Percentage of shares outstanding on loan, stock-loan utilisation rate and average stock-loan fee for Volkswagen AG ordinary shares around the event date (day 0)

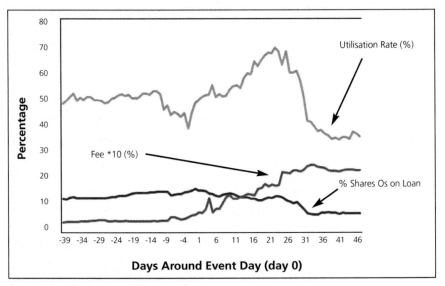

Source: Data Explorers and Thomson Reuters

By examining stock-lending data around the time of the alleged manipulation, I observe that the ordinary shares experienced an exceptional price increase, followed by a reduction in shares on loan, and finally a gradual price reversal. This is consistent with the pattern of 'pump, squeeze and dump' that I use to define an 'apparent manipulative short squeeze'.

In terms of stock characteristics, Volkswagen had a large market capitalisation, limited free float and a high days-to-cover ratio. Trading volume was elevated and stock-return volatility increased sharply in the days before the event day. As such, the stock's characteristics match those from my sample of apparent manipulative shot squeezes in all but one respect – namely, that Volkswagen was a large-cap stock.

The stock-loan utilisation rate was high at 49.02% on the event day and rose in the days afterwards (to 55.96% by the fifth day after the event day). The stock-loan fee also rose, from 0.68% on the event day to 0.76% by the fifth day afterwards and to 1.40% by the tenth day. Thus, the pattern observed is also consistent with the pattern tested earlier using four dummy variables as a robustness check.

There is the added complication of trading in options as well as ordinary shares, and this makes the case study richer than the manipulation that I describe. The behaviour of Porsche AG would only be deemed to be manipulation if the firm's *intention* was to manipulate the ordinary shares of Volkswagen AG. This may never be known, and it is this feature that makes the study of alleged stock manipulation a challenging task.

CHAPTER 6

FINAL THOUGHTS

In this book I have looked at a number of phenomena that lead security prices to move temporarily away from equilibrium. These situations present traders with opportunities to earn profits and can provide the lifeblood for many a trading desk.

For those who are caught unaware and forced to close their positions at unfavourable prices, these episodes can also prove costly.

Do these deviations in securities prices matter to traditional, long-only investors?

For an investor managing an unleveraged, closed-ended fund with a long-term horizon, perhaps they are of little import. However, the volatility associated with these phenomena *can* provide opportunities for building long-term positions at attractive cost bases. Volatility can also play on the emotions of an investor, making it difficult for him to hold onto losing positions, despite their apparent long-term attractiveness.

Both traders and investors are strongly armed when they can combine a good estimate of a security's fair value (perhaps obtained through fundamental analysis) with an awareness of the phenomena that can move security prices away from recent equilibrium levels. With a good fair-value estimate, one can assess the risks of strategic trading for any given security price level. This book presents some new evidence on phenomena such as crowded exits, index-fund predation and manipulation against short sellers that should assist traders in assessing opportunities and risks.

Flexibility

Flexibility is important to traders, in two ways. First, a flexible mandate allows a trader to operate across many markets. This creates a large opportunity set, and allows for the exploitation of cross-market anomalies. There is a fair amount of evidence that it is difficult to consistently outperform within a single, mature or developed market. But across markets, where fewer market participants operate and where market segmentation prevents some others from exploiting anomalies, it should be possible to find greater trading opportunities. Of course, having too great an opportunity set can overburden a single trader, but teams can be used to cope with such problems.

Secondly, flexibility helps prevents traders from becoming predictable in their actions. Predictable behaviour should be avoided wherever possible. Many of the trading opportunities discussed in this book arise because of the predictable trading of certain market players. These include full-replication index funds who become the victim of front running, price-momentum traders who become the victim of trade-based manipulation and those using rigid risk-management systems whose actions can be read in advance and exploited by astute observers.

Predatory trading

Predatory trading exploits knowledge about the strategies and positions of other market participants. In particular, the predator trades in such a way as to benefit from the market impact of forced transactions by the prey. Predatory trading is suited to traders who can take both long and short positions, and who are relatively unconstrained by benchmarks or risk-management systems. It is most profitable in markets with poor liquidity and where a forced trader's position is large relative to the capacity of predators. Predation is most intense when there are fewer predators, or when predators collude and act as one.

A perfect predator would be flexible (i.e. able to operate across many markets), strong (i.e. well-capitalised compared to the prey) and knowledgeable about the capital, positions and strategies of others in the market.

Ethics

By examining legal and regulatory evidence, comments from both industry bodies and experienced practitioners and the results of tests using an ethical-evaluation matrix, it is possible to arrive at an opinion on the ethics of predatory trading. Predatory trading is ethical when it is based on publicly-available or inferable information; when the predators are truthful in their dealings with others; and when the predator firm's clients are not harmed. Predatory trading is unethical if it harms the firm's own clients; if the predator is untruthful about his activities; or if the information driving the strategy is obtained through a breach of a firewall.

Forced traders

Traders employing explicit or implicit leverage must take extreme care to limit the risk that they become forced traders. Where a market participant is *forced* to de-lever, perhaps because of a margin call that he cannot meet, he becomes vulnerable to exploitation by others. Becoming a victim of predatory trading can be costly; even terminal. Where possible, risk management systems should be flexible and somewhat confidential in nature, to reduce the risk of predatory trading. This is not always practical, though – investment consultants and trustees can be sceptical about allocating money to a manager who is unable or unwilling to describe his risk management process.

It is important for traders to understand the ecology of markets. Just as you can become a victim by trading predictably, so a good knowledge of the predictable behaviour of others can present opportunities for profit. Awareness of the types of actor operating in a market and an understanding of their strategies can be valuable.

Market data, such as stock-lending data, and inferable knowledge, such as the cost basis of short-sellers or the capital strength and positions of a rival fund, can be used to highlight specific trading opportunities.

Only the paranoid survive

Facts about your own market positions, cost basis, margin arrangements and capital strength can also be valuable to others – you make up part of the market eco-system! It is sensible to exercise mild paranoia with respect to information about your own portfolio and capital resources. Remember that those who serve you, such as brokers and custodians, will hold information that others could find useful. This valuable information might be swapped in social settings and could be used against you in future. It should be protected as best as possible.

Ever-changing cycles

Traders should be alert to Niederhoffer's notion of "ever-changing cycles". Any observed regularity in a market is unlikely to remain unnoticed for long. As academics or industry analysts publish the results of empirical studies and identify trading strategies that worked in prior periods, traders respond to the new information and attempt to exploit the identified phenomena. As a result of this process, the ecology of the market develops over time and trading rules that worked well for many years can stop working or even go dramatically into reverse. Traders must continuously analyse and re-assess patterns that they believe to be exploitable. The dynamics and ecology of a market rarely stand still.

Short selling

Short-sellers experience an array of risks that can differ from those faced by long-investors. These include liquidity problems such as crowded exits. Where short-sellers hold large positions relative to normal trading volume, and when a catalyst prompts short-sellers to cover their positions rapidly and simultaneously, the temporary excess of demand for stock relative to normal trading volume leads to upward pressure on the stock price. Crowded exits are associated with statistically significant, positive abnormal returns.

The distribution of stock returns is influenced by the 'crowdedness' of short positions: stocks with higher short interest in any given month exhibit greater return skew the next month. Should short-sellers be particularly concerned if securities prices temporarily surge upwards against their expectations? Yes, as the *path of stock returns* is important to some market players, including traders who are liable to margin calls and managers of open-ended funds who can suffer client redemptions. A temporary market imbalance can lead to a *permanent loss* where a trader is unable to hold on to a losing position.

Crowded exits can create path-dependency problems for short-sellers and this risk should be mitigated. Traders are advised to exercise caution when short-selling smaller, less liquid stocks with high days-to-cover ratios. Also, given that crowded exits can last for several days, short-sellers should cover their short positions immediately upon observing exceptional levels of covering by other shorts-sellers in crowded positions. There is a time lag between the start of a crowded exit and the release of public data that would confirm exceptional short covering. Stock lending market colour thus becomes important to a short-seller, providing a timely advantage over others relying simply on publicly-released data.

Manipulation

Manipulation against short-sellers can take the form of price manipulation combined with action-based manipulation in the form of a securities loan recall. I find that manipulative short squeezes are rare events, at least for the sample of data examined. However, where they do occur, short-sellers experience significant losses. These are followed by a price reversal, but short-sellers who have covered their positions do not benefit from this effect. It is difficult to forecast short squeezes from an analysis of size, liquidity, volatility and trading volume alone, as these early warning indicators generate many false signals.

A short-seller who fears manipulative short squeezes can mitigate this risk by paying additional fees to borrow securities on a term basis, or by over-borrowing to provide a buffer against partial loan recall. Both of these techniques incur a cost but reduce the risk of becoming the victim of a manipulative short squeeze.

Stop losses

Short-sellers also face the timing problem known as synchronisation risk as well as the potential for (theoretically) unlimited losses. Both of these risks can be addressed by employing stop losses. Although there is no evidence that the use of stop losses boosts risk-adjusted returns for long investors, they can be a sensible tool for short-sellers. However, the rigid use of stop losses can open a trader up to predation risk, where others know the trader's cost basis and stop-loss rule. Perhaps the use of fuzzy stop losses, with grey (loosely-defined) thresholds, or some element of unpredictable behaviour can be useful here – the stop-loss rule should contain just enough uncertainty to foil the predators!

Flexibility, an awareness of the changing nature of the market ecology and an understanding of the usefulness but also limitations of risk-management systems can prove valuable tools for traders competing in markets. While these are not sufficient for guaranteeing trading success, they should at least minimise the possibility that a trader falls victim to predatory trading or to path-dependency problems such as crowded exits.

APPENDIX 1

THE MARKET MODEL

According to Fama (1976) the market model is specified as:

$$R_{it} = a_i + b_i R_{mt} + e_{it} \qquad (1)$$

where R_{it} is the rate or return of the ith security at event day t and R_{mt} is the rate of return of the FTSE All Share Index at time t.[37] The abnormal return of the ith security at event day t is estimated as, $AR_{it} = R_{it} - \hat{R}_{it}$ where $\hat{R}_{it} = \hat{a}_i - \hat{\beta}_i R_{mt}$ and $\hat{a}, \hat{\beta}$ are ordinary least-square estimates of the market model parameters over the period t = −360 to t = − 40 trading days relative to the review day. The statistical significance of the average abnormal return (AAR) and the cumulative average abnormal returns (CAAR) for a sample of N companies for the event day t is assessed using standard event methodology techniques.

---

[37] The share return is derived from the Datastream Return Index (Datatype "RI").

APPENDIX 2

ABNORMAL RETURNS

Abnormal returns for company i are calculated as:

$$AR_{it} = R_{it} - \hat{R}_{it} \tag{2}$$

where AR_{it} is the abnormal rate or return of the $_i th$ security at event day t, R_{it} is the rate or return of the ith security at event day t, and $\hat{R}_{it}$ is the estimated return generated by the market model (Equation 1) and estimated as follows.

$$\hat{R}_{it} = \hat{a}_i + \hat{\beta}_i R_{mt} \tag{3}$$

Substituting (3) into (2) abnormal returns are calculated as follows:

$$AR_{it} = R_{it} - (\hat{\alpha}_i + \hat{\beta}_i R_{mt}) \tag{4}$$

The cumulative abnormal returns for company i over period t1 to t2, where (t1< t2) is:

$$CAR_{i,(t_1,t_2)} = \sum_{t=t_1}^{t_2} AR_{it} \tag{5}$$

The average abnormal return (AAR) at time t for a number of N companies is calculated as in Equation 6.

$$AAR_t - \frac{1}{N} \sum_{i=1}^{N} AR_{it} \tag{6}$$

To test the statistical significance of average abnormal returns for a group of N companies we use standard statistical techniques as proposed by various researchers (Seith and Warner, 1980, Armitage, 1996). More specifically we use the following equation.

$$Z_t (AAR_{it}) = \sqrt{N} \; \frac{\sum_{i=1}^{N} SAR_{it}}{N} \qquad \sim \; N(0,1) \tag{8}$$

where

$$SAR_{it} = \frac{AR_{it}}{se(AR_{it})} \tag{9}$$

and

$$se\left(AR_{it}\right) = s_i^2 \left[1 + \frac{1}{N} + \frac{\left(R_{mt} - \bar{R}_m\right)^2}{(N-1)Var\left(R_m\right)}\right]$$

(10)

where

S_i is the standard error of the regression estimating alpha and beta

N is the number of observations in the estimation period

$\bar{R}_m$ is the mean market return in the estimation period

R_{mt} is the return on the market in the test period

$Var\left(R_{mt}\right)$ is the variance of the return of the market in the estimation period.

The cumulative average abnormal return for N companies over period t1 to t2, where (t1< t2) is measured with equation 7.

$$CAAR_{i,(t_1,t_2)} = \sum_{t=t_1}^{t_2} AAR_{it}$$

(11)

The statistical significance of CAARs are estimated by estimating the z-statistic of equation (12).

$$z = \bar{w}\sqrt{N} \quad \sim \quad N(0,1)$$

(12)

where

$$\bar{w} = \frac{1}{N}\sum_{i=1}^{N} w_i$$

(13)

and

$$wi\left(t_1,t_2\right) = \frac{\sum_{t_1}^{t_2} SAR_{it}}{\sqrt{t_2 - t_1 + 1}}$$

(14)

BIBLIOGRAPHY

Abreu, D. and Brunnermeier, M., 2002, 'Synchronization Risk and Delayed Arbitrage', *Journal of Financial Economics*, 66 (2-3), 341-360.

Arthur, W.B., Holland, J., LeBaron, B., Palmer, R., and Taylor, P., 1997, [agent-based modelling in financial markets] in *The Economy as an Evolving Complex System, Vol. II*.eds. Arthur, W.B., Durlauf, S., and Lane, D. Addison-Wesley, Reading MA, USA.

Asquith, P., Pathak, P.A and Ritter, J.R., 2005. 'Short Interest, Institutional Ownership and Stock Returns', *Journal of Financial Economics*, 78, 243-276.

Attari, M., Mello, A.S. and Ruckes, M.E., 2005, 'Arbitraging Arbitrageurs'. *Journal of Finance*, 60 (5), 2471-2511.

Barberis, N., Huang, M. and Santos, T., 2001, 'Prospect Theory and Asset Prices', *Quarterly Journal of Economics*, 116, 1-53.

Beneish, M. and Whaley, R., 1996, 'An anatomy of the "S&P game": The effects of changing the rules', *Journal of Finance*, Vol. 51, p.p. 1909-1930.

Bentson, G.J. and Wood, R.A., 2006, 'Why Effective Spreads on NASDAQ were Higher than on the New York Stock Exchange' (Conference Proceedings), *Journal of Banking and Finance Conference*, Beijing, June 2006.

Bernstein, P., 1998, 'Why the Efficient Market Offers Hope to Active Management', in *Economics and Portfolio Strategy*. Peter Bernstein, Inc., New York, NY, USA.

Black, F., 1986, 'Noise', *Journal of Finance*, 41 (3), 529-543.

Blitzer, D. and Dash, S., 2004, *Index Effect Revisited*, Standard and Poor's, New York, NY, USA.

Boehmer, E., Jones, C.M. and Zhang, X., 2008, 'Which Shorts are Informed?' *Journal of Finance*, 63 (2), 491-527.

Bowie N.B., 1998, 'Kantian Theory of Capitalism', *Business Ethics Quarterly*, Ruffin Series Special Issue No 1.

Brown, P., Chappel, N., Da Silva Rosa, R. and Walter, T., 2002, 'The Reach of the Disposition Effect: Large Sample Evidence across Investor Classes', Working Paper, The University of Western Australia.

Brunnermeier, M.K. and Nagel, S., 2004. Hedge Funds and the Technology Bubble. *Journal of Finance*, 59 (5), 2013-2040.

Brunnermeier, M.K. and Pedersen, L.H., 2005, 'Predatory Trading', *Journal of Finance*, 60 (4), 1825-1863.

Cai, F., 2003. 'Was There Front Running During the LTCM Crisis?' *FRB International Finance Discussion Paper No. 758*. Available at SSRN: http://ssrn.com/abstract=385560 or DOI: 10.2139/ssrn.385560

CFA Institute, 2005, *Standards of Practice Handbook*, 9th Edition, Charlottesville, VA, USA.

Chen, H., Noronha, G. and Singh, V., 2006, 'Index Changes and Losses to Index Fund Investors', *Financial Analysts Journal*, 62 (4), 31-47.

Cici, G., 2005. 'The Impact of the Disposition Effect on the Performance of Mutual Funds', Working Paper, Wharton Research Data Services.

Cohen, L., Diether, K.B. and Malloy, C.J., 2007, 'Supply and Demand Shifts in the Shorting Market', *Journal of Finance*, 62 (5), 2061-2096.

Coval, J.D. and Shumway, T, 2001, 'Do Behavioral Biases Affect Prices?', Working Paper, University of Michigan.

Coval, J.D. and Stafford, E., 2007, 'Asset Fire Sales (and Purchases) in Equity Markets', *Journal of Financial Economics*, 86 (2), 479-512.

D'Avolio, G., 2002. 'The Market for Borrowing Stock', *Journal of Financial Economics*, 66 (2-3), 271-306.

Da Silva Rosa, R., To, H.M. and Walter, T., 2005, 'Evidence Contrary to the Disposition Effect Amongst UK-Managed Funds', Working Paper, the University of Western Australia.

Dechow, P.M., Hutton, A.P., Meulbroek, L. and Sloan, R.G., 2001, 'Short Sellers, Fundamental Analysis, and Stock Returns', *Journal of Financial Economics*, 61, 77-106.

DeLong, J.B., Schleifer A., Summers, L.H. and Waldman, R.J., 1990, 'Positive Feedback Investment Strategies and Destabilizing Rational Speculation', *Journal of Finance*, 45 (2), 375-395.

Dhar, R. and Zhu, N., 2008. 'Up Close and Personal: An Individual Level Analysis of the Disposition Effect', Working Paper, Yale School of Management.

Diether, K.B., Lee K.H. and Werner, I.M., 2009. 'Short-sale Strategies and Return Predictability', *Review of Financial Studies*, 22 (2), 575-607.

Dobson J., 2005, 'Monkey Business: A neo-Darwinist Approach to Ethics Codes'," *Financial Analysts Journal*, 61 (3), 59-64.

Donaldson T. and Dunfee, T.W., 1994, 'Toward a Unified Conception of Business Ethics: Integrative Social Contracts Theory', *Academy of Management Review*, 19 (2), 252-284.

Dow, J. and Gorton, G., 2006, 'Noise Traders', National Bureau of Economic Research, Working Paper 12256.

Duffie, D., Garleanu, N. and Pedersen, L.H., 2002, 'Securities Lending, Shorting and Pricing', *Journal of Financial Economics*, 66 (2-3), 307-339.

Farmer, J. D. and Lo, A.W., 1999, 'Frontiers of Finance: Evolution and Efficient Markets', Proceedings of the National Academy of Science USA, Vol. 96, 9991-9992, August 1999.

Fisher C. and Lovell, A., 2006, *Business Ethics and Values. Individual, Corporate and International Perspectives*. Second Edition, Prentice Hall.

Friedman, M., 1953, 'The Methodology of Positive Economics', in Friedman, *Essays in Positive Economics*. University of Chicago Press, Chicago, IL, USA.

Gamboa-Cavazos, M, and Savor, P., 2007, 'Holding On to Your Shorts: When Do Short-Sellers Retreat?', Harvard University Working Paper.

Garvey, R. and Murphy, A., 2004, 'Are Professional Traders Too Slow to Realize their Losses?', *Financial Analysts Journal*, 60 (4), 35-43.

Geczy, C.C., Musto, D.K. and Reed, A.V., 2002, 'Stocks are Special Too: an Analysis of the Equity Lending Market', *Journal of Financial Economics*, 66 (2-3), 241-269.

Gemmill, G. and Thomas, D.C., 2002, 'Noise Trading, Costly Arbitrage and Asset Pricing: Evidence from Closed-End Funds,' *Journal of Finance*, 57, 2571-2594.

Grinblatt, M. and Han, B., 2004, 'Prospect Theory, Mental Accounting, and Momentum', Working Paper, UCLA.

Hardie, I. and MacKenzie, D., 2007, 'Assembling an Economic Actor: the Agencement of a Hedge Fund', *The Sociological Review*, 55 (1), 57-80.

Henry T.R. and Koski, J.L., 2008, 'Short Selling Around Seasoned Equity Offerings', Working Paper, University of Georgia.

Hirshleifer, D. and Luo, G, 2001, 'On the Survival of Overconfident Traders in a Competitive Securities Market', *Journal of Financial Markets*, 4, 73-84.

Irvine, P.J. and Sivakumar, K., 2005, 'Liquidity and Asset Prices: the Case of the Short Squeeze and Returns to Short Positions', Working Paper, University of Georgia.

Jacobs, B.I. and Levy, K.N., 2007, '20 Myths about Enhanced Active 120-20 Strategies', *Financial Analysts Journal*, 63 (4), 19-26.

Jegadeesh, N. and Titman, S., 1993, 'Returns to Buying Winners and Selling Losers: Implications for Stock Market Efficiency', *Journal of Finance*, 48 (1), 65-91.

Jegadeesh, N. and Titman, S., 2001, 'Profitability of Momentum Strategies: an Evaluation of Alternative Explanations', *Journal of Finance*, 56 (2), 699-720.

Jiang, G., Mahoney, P.G. and Mei, J., 2005, 'Market Manipulation: A Comprehensive Study of Stock Pools', *Journal of Financial Economics*, 77, 147-170.

Kahneman, D. and Tversky, A., 1979, 'Prospect Theory: An Analysis of Decision Under Risk', *Econometrica*, 47 (2), 263-291.

Keim, D.B., 1999, 'An Analysis of Mutual Fund Design: the Case of Investing in Small-Cap Stocks', *Journal of Financial Economics*, 51, 173-194.

Khwaja, A.I. and Mian A. 2005, 'Unchecked Intermediaries: Price Manipulation in an Emerging Market', *Journal of Financial Economics*, 78 (1), 203-241.

Krapels, E., 2001, 'Re-examining the Metallgesellschaft Affair and its Implications for Oil Traders', *Oil and Gas Journal*, 26 March 2001.

Lev, B. and Nissim, D., 2006, 'The Persistence of the Accruals Anomaly', *Contemporary Accounting Research*, 23 (1), 193-226.

Lo, A.W., 2004, 'The Adaptive Markets Hypothesis', *Journal of Portfolio Management*, 30, 15-29.

Locke, P. and Mann, S.C., 2000, 'Do Professional Traders Exhibit Loss-Realization Aversion?', Working Paper, George Washington University

Lorenzo V.D., 2006, 'Does the law encourage unethical conduct in the securities industry?', *Fordham Journal of Corporate and Financial Law*, 11, 765-805.

Luetge C., 2005, 'Economic Ethics, Business Ethics and the Idea of Mutual Advantages', *Business Ethics; a European Review*, 14 (2), 108-118.

Lynch, A. and Mendenhall, R., 1997, 'New Evidence of Stock Price Effects Associated With Changes in the S&P 500 Index', *Journal of Business*, 70, 351-383.

MacIntyre, A., 1987, *After Virtue: a Study in Moral Theory*, Duckworth, London, UK.

MacKenzie, D.A., 2006, *An Engine, Not a Camera: How Financial Models Shape Markets*, Inside Technology, MIT Press, Cambridge, MA, USA.

Macquarie, 2009, *Risky Business: Stop the Losses, Take the Profits*, Macquarie Research, London, UK.

Mahoney, P.G., 1999, 'The Stock Pools and the Securities Exchange Act', *Journal of Financial Economics*, 51, 343-369.

McCosh, A., 1999, *Financial Ethics*, Kluwer Academic Publishers, London, UK.

Miller, E.M., 1977, 'Risk, Uncertainty and Divergence of Opinion', *Journal of Finance*, 32 (4), 1151-1168.

Nagel, S., 2005, 'Short-Sales, Institutional Investors and the Cross-Section of Stock Returns', *Journal of Financial Economics*, 78 (2), 277-309.

Niederhoffer, V., 1997, *The Education of a Speculator*, John Wiley and Sons, Inc., New York, NY, USA.

Odean, T., 1998, 'Are Investors Reluctant to Realize their Losses?' *Journal of Finance*, 53, 1775-1798.

Ofek, E., Richardson, M. and Whitelaw, R.F. 2004, 'Limited Arbitrage and Short Sale Restrictions: Evidence from the Options Market', *Journal of Financial Economics*, 74, 305-342.

Ormerod, P., 2005, *Why Most Things Fail*, Faber and Faber Limited, London, UK.

Ross, S.A., 1976, 'The Arbitrage Theory of Capital Asset Pricing', *Journal of Economic Theory*, 13 (3), 341-360.

Safieddine, A. and Wilhelm, W.J., 1996, 'An Empirical Investigation of Short-Selling Activity Prior to Seasoned Equity Offerings', *Journal of Finance*, 51 (2), 729-749.

Schneider, P.A.D., 2000, 'The Demise of Ethical Monism', *Online Journal of Ethics University of St. Thomas Huston*, 3 (1).

Sharpe, W.F., 1964, 'Capital Asset Prices: A Theory of Market Equilibrium Under Conditions of Risk', *Journal of Finance*, 19, 425-442.

Shefrin, H. and Statman, M., 1985, 'The Disposition to Sell Winners Too Early and Ride Losers Too Long: Theory and Evidence', *Journal of Finance*, 40, 777-790.

Shkilko, A., Van Ness, B. and Van Ness, R., 2008, 'Price-destabilizing Short-Selling', Working Paper, Wilfrid Laurier University.

Shleifer, A. and Vishny, R., 1992, 'Liquidation Values and Debt Capacity: A Market Equilibrium Approach', *Journal of Finance*, 47, 1343-1366.

Shleifer, A. and Vishny, R., 1997, 'The Limits of Arbitrage', *Journal of Finance*, 52 (1), 35-55.

Siegel, J.J. and Schwartz, J.D., 2006, 'Long-Term Returns on the Original S&P 500 Companies', *Financial Analysts Journal*, 62 (1), 18-31.

Szego, G., 2006, 'Financial Regulation, Why and How?' (Conference Proceedings), *Journal of Banking and Finance 30th Anniversary Conference*, Beijing, China June 6-8 2006.

Thaler, R., 1985, 'Mental Accounting and Consumer Choice', *Marketing Science*, 4, 199-214.

Toenjes, R.H., 2002, 'Why be Moral in Business? A Rawlsian Approach to Moral Motivation', *Business Ethics Quarterly*, 12, (1).

Velasquez M. and Brady, F.N., 1997, 'Catholic Natural Law and Business Ethics', *Business Ethics Quarterly*, 7 (2).

Wilson, E., 1975, *Sociobiology: the New Synthesis*, Belknap Press of Harvard University, Cambridge, MA, USA.

Wu, J., 2008, 'Short-Selling and the Informational Efficiency of Prices', Working Paper, Mays Business School, Texas A&M University.

Yu, F., 2006, 'How Profitable is Capital Structure Arbitrage?', *Financial Analysts Journal*, 62 (5), 47-62.

Zaloom, C., 2006, *Out of the Pits: Traders and Technology from Chicago to London*, University of Chicago Press, Chicago, IL, USA.

INDEX

3Com 29

A

ABN Amro 46-47

adaptive markets hypothesis 21

agent-based modelling 20

arbitrage 5-16, 21-30, 48-49, 89, 97-
102, 119-121, 130-133, 143-146,
171-172

   arbitrage theory of capital asset
pricing 5-6

   capital-structure opportunity 22-26

   delayed arbitrage 12

   expected returns and risks 23

   social dimension 15-16

asset pricing 4-7

   capital asset pricing model 6, 93

B

Barclays 24-26

bonds 3

Brunnermeier and Pedersen model 42-
44, 48, 77

bubbles 13, 16

C

cash flow 3-6, 140

Citigroup 137-138

clients 10-12, 39, 49-50, 78-79, 105-
106, 181

corporate bonds 4

cross-market trading 22-23

   anomalies 23

crowded exit

   causes 87-88

   crowded position 90

   example 83

   short cover 95-100

D

days-to-cover ratio (DCR) 90-94, 100,
174

discount rate 3-6

divergence xi, 15, 19, 107-108,

dotcom bubble 13-14, 17

E

ecology of markets 17-21

ethics of predatory trading 65, 181

   chinese walls 78

   consequentialist perspective 71

   contractualism 72-73

   framework 73-79

   law 68-69

   regulators 66-68

   virtue ethics 70-71

F

fair value 4-5

Financial Services Authority (FSA) 25-

26, 140, 66-68, 137-138

fundamental-versus-price comparator
investors 16

front-running 50-51

G

Goldman Sachs Asset Management
41-42

H

hedge funds 11-15, 17, 22, 40, 42

I

index-fund revision 60-63 (*see also*:
predatory trading opportunities, S&P
500 index reviews; predatory trading
opportunities, FTSE 350)

index-fund predation 36-39, 49-50,
64-65

informed rational speculators 16

L

leveraged trader (*see*: predatory
trading opportunities, distressed
participants)

liquidity 33

loan covenants 34

long-only investors 179

Long-Term Capital Management
(LTCM) 45

losses
    book losses response 121-127
    realising losses 117-120

M

mandatory convertible notes (MCNs)
24-26

manipulation 137-138, 183-184
    action-based 141-142
    case studies 145-149
    identifying 142-145
    information-based 140
    shorts 150-155
    short squeeze 156-170
    trade-based 138-139

margin calls 15, 33-34

Metallgesellschaft AG 37-38

models 4-6, 17-18, 20-21, 42 (*see also*:
Brunnermeier and Pedersen model;
asset pricing, capital asset pricing
model)

N

noise traders 7-14